MW01290243

Roaming Free Inside the Cage

A Daoist Approach to the Enneagram and Spiritual Transformation

William M. Schafer Ph.D.

iUniverse, Inc.
New York Bloomington

Roaming Free Inside the Cage
A Daoist Approach to the Enneagram and Spiritual Transformation

Copyright © 2009 William M. Schafer Ph.D.

All rights reserved. No part of this book may be used or reproduced by any means, graphic, electronic, or mechanical, including photocopying, recording, taping or by any information storage retrieval system without the written permission of the publisher except in the case of brief quotations embodied in critical articles and reviews.

iUniverse books may be ordered through booksellers or by contacting:

iUniverse
1663 Liberty Drive
Bloomington, IN 47403
www.iuniverse.com
1-800-Authors (1-800-288-4677)

Because of the dynamic nature of the Internet, any Web addresses or links contained in this book may have changed since publication and may no longer be valid. The views expressed in this work are solely those of the author and do not necessarily reflect the views of the publisher, and the publisher hereby disclaims any responsibility for them.

ISBN: 978-1-4401-8862-6 (pbk)
ISBN: 978-1-4401-8864-0 (cloth)
ISBN: 978-1-4401-8863-3 (ebook)

Printed in the United States of America

iUniverse rev. date: 12/22/09

To Sally, whose lovely face I have glimpsed in the stillness she left behind.

Contents

PART I: THE ROOTS

The Developmental Structure of Type

PART II: THE TRUNK

The Self-Maintaining Nature of Type

PART III: THE CANOPY

Living Freely Within Type

PART IV: THE COSMIC TREE

Exploring the Human Condition

Acknowledgments

The longer I teach, the clearer it becomes that very little of what I teach originates within me. This book owes whatever wisdom it contains to a myriad of teachers, mentors, friends, clients, and students. Among my many teachers over the years one is particularly important to this book. David Daniels freely offered both his valuable time and vast knowledge of the Enneagram as he went over the text with me chapter by chapter. Special thanks are also due to those who helped bring the book to fruition: from old friend, Mike Leach, editor emeritus at Orbis Books who first told me to publish it, to new friends, Caroline Myss, who tried valiantly to hawk the manuscript to established publishing houses despite the current economic crisis, and Jeanne Ballew, whose thoughtful editing so often saved me from myself. In the end, however, it is to Alice, my wife, that the greatest thanks are due. Lover, friend, teacher, and muse I learn more spending one day with you than I do reading all of the books on my shelves.

List of Figures and Tables

Foreword

In this pioneering contribution to Enneagram theory, Bill Schafer brings the wisdom of Daoism to the Enneagram understandings. He thus helps us better appreciate the universal nature of the Enneagram, how its fundamental structure is found everywhere in the world, and why we find the nine Enneagram patterns or types in all cultures.

The Enneagram's understandings emphasize integration of our essential qualities into our lives; that is, they ask us to integrate and balance all of our differentiated parts. In trying to do this, we don't seek to get rid of personality, but rather we become open to infusing it with our higher or essential qualities that have always been there. We do this because we realize that essence has not gone away from us; we have gone away from it. And Bill in his elegant, clear, deeply moving and even poetic style brings all of this home to us when he writes "Daoism's basic credo is that Dao cannot be found existing by itself. It is always hidden within the particular, so when you seek the Absolute all by itself, you are looking in the wrong place."

The original state of essence as seen in all infants—as Bill puts it, a state of presence, shared awareness, and joy—naturally goes into the background as personality structure develops in order to adapt to the external material world. Working with the Enneagram provides a structure for reclaiming the essential qualities with which we were born. Bill puts it this way, "We do not own or control the energy needed for spiritual growth. It is there, free for the asking. It resides within the quiet willingness to simply observe." For each type, he describes how to access this energy in the pivot of the Dao, a practice that can help release the imbalances of energy that constrict our hearts and minds.

Another major contribution of Bill's work is his description of how the Daoist understanding of the three manifestations of *Qi*, or life force (as *yin* or receptive/passive energy, *yang* or active/assertive energy, and *yin/yang* or the reconciling/balancing of the two) interact with the three *dan tian* (what we in the West call the three centers of intelligence), thus forming the nine Enneagram types. In this view, the three centers of experience and three manifestations of life force are shown as three equilateral triangles of body, heart, and head types. I call this the three centers approach, wherein each person has access to all three manifestations of *Qi* and all three *dan tian*, that is, all three expressions of energy and all three centers of intelligence. As Bill points out, this provides each type with balance from the point of view of both energy and its manner of expression. In addition, he provides thoughtful insights into how each of these triangles can either devolve into contracted expression or develop into greater freedom.

Notwithstanding these new additions to the theory, there are many similarities between Bill's approach and the Narrative Tradition. Bill shows us how the three forms of *Qi* become constricted or contracted and unbalanced during personality formation into the nine types. He then sets out the path of healing and release from the contractions of type through allowing in the experience of the feared avoidance. This is similar to our teachings in the Narrative Tradition where the types speak for themselves. Our teachings focus on the conversion of the passion or driving emotion of type back into the higher essence qualities of type, on the process of integration of personality, and on bringing the higher qualities of type back into our lives. Bill's approach seeks to gain freedom through facing our deepest avoidances or fears in the stillness of the *daoshu,* or the Pivot of Dao. The pivot is the "frictionless point of non-resistance at the very center of the wheel where the seemingly opposed forces of the wheel's circumference unite. Its power resides precisely in its lack of resistance." This is quite compatible with the Narrative Tradition's process of befriending personal reactivity in order to discover our deepest concerns or avoidances and our fundamental early beliefs or traps associated with our now largely anachronistic adaptive strategies.

There is much in Bill's work to digest and absorb: principles and practices, history, symbolism, and poetic expression. For instance, Bill describes the ultimate value of the Enneagram thus: "It is a window that shows you your own human face even as it opens your heart and mind to a deeper vision of the cosmic reality in which you are a necessary and principal participant." This work requires only the caution that, as in much that is written about the Enneagram, we are dealing with subjective internal experience rather than objective external measurement. It is a book on *experience of* rather than *knowledge about.* So do come to it with a willingness to use the principles of optimal learning: be receptive and grounded in order to open your heart and mind with curiosity, and have the expectation of benefit. Then you will indeed benefit greatly from this fundamental, deep and penetrating work on the Enneagram and the Dao.

David Daniels, M.D., September 2009
Clinical Professor
Dept. of Psychiatry and Behavioral Science
Stanford Medical School

Preface

I first heard of the Enneagram (pronounced EN-ee-a-gram) from Alice. (She and I were later married, and we are very happy together, but I can't guarantee such good fortune to every reader.) We had just begun dating when she gave me Helen Palmer's book *The Enneagram: Understanding Yourself and the Others in Your Life*. She said it had been invaluable to her in coming to a better relationship with her son, whom she had been raising alone after the death of her husband. I put the book up on the shelf of things to be read on a rainy day. Several months later, Alice called off our relationship, and we stopped seeing each other. The book remained with me.

One rainy Michigan fall day, I opened it. Alice had told me I was probably a Type Four, but being a somewhat compulsive reader, I started the book at the beginning rather than turning to the chapter on Fours, which lay buried somewhere in the back third of the book. I was immediately put off by the introduction. I was a psychoanalytically trained clinical psychologist. My specialties were infant and toddler development, attachment theory, and infant mental health. I was by no means your bread and butter American psychologist engrossed in pointer readings and behavior modification, but I was accustomed to a certain language and style of empirical research. To be sure, I possessed a fascination with subjective experience (my doctoral dissertation had been on the development of the sense of self in infancy), but I simultaneously distrusted theories and treatment methods that did not offer at least the pretense of being grounded in experimental research. The first sixty-five pages of Palmer's book were filled with descriptions of peculiar (to me) concepts like essence, chief feature, higher mind, passions, virtues, and emotional and belly centers of intelligence. The ideas seemed unfamiliar, slippery, hard to pin down, and impossible to remember. My first reaction was to dismiss most of it as New Age woo-woo.

But I kept on reading. (The less I liked the book, the more determined I grew to prove Alice wrong.) I finally came to Type Four. I could identify Alice's son in the descriptions, but I did not see myself. Type Five came next, and I recognized Alice immediately. Next came Type Six. By this time, my mind had settled into a routine and rather familiar state of quiet argument with the author: "How do you know that? Where is your evidence? How can you be so sure? There are surely other ways to explain that!" I was so accustomed to this state that I was not even aware of it—until I started reading Palmer's description of the doubting mind and saw myself simultaneously doubting what I was reading. As I turned the next few pages about worst case scenario thinking, I watched myself imagining what awful things would befall me if indeed I were one of those people who habitually assumed the worst. Finally, I found myself putting off agreement with the section on delaying action in favor of more analysis until I had time to read other authors on the subject! My reaction to Helen's chapter on Type Six, the Devil's Advocate as she called it in those days, was immediate and intense. I wondered how someone who had never met me could know so much about me. I felt viscerally ill. It was as though some unknown observer had peered deeper into my being than I myself could see. My second reaction lay just behind the first and was more soothing. For the first time in my life, I felt that there was an inner coherence to my confusing list of traits, quirks, flaws, and talents. My triumphs and failures were not a random patchwork produced by a demented weaver. Once I could see how my point of view, my dominant emotional state, and the way I paid attention to, remembered, and organized things made the world seem as it did, the many twists and turns of my life all began to make sense even though they had so often produced results I had neither foreseen nor intended.

Later, when Alice and I resumed dating, I told her I was a Six for sure. She went to her room to read the chapter. A half hour later she returned with the book and said, "Bill, that's pathetic." Her smile and subsequent hug told me she was nonetheless glad she now had some way to understand me.

The Enneagram's first practical use was to help us weather our initial years living together. Today we both are convinced that without it we probably would never have stayed together. I then began using the Enneagram in my clinical work. I didn't talk about it or recommend it, but I used it as a diagnostic template. I wasn't interested in determining whether a given client was a Nine or a Two, a Seven or an Eight, but I was getting in the habit of listening to a particular story or interaction with the help of a little voice in my head murmuring "that sounds very much like a Type such and such dilemma, doesn't it?" Meanwhile, I was reading everything I could find on the Enneagram. Gradually, I began teaching it to my students and supervisees. I found most of them were puzzled by it at first and then excited and eager to know more. Group supervision with clinicians came to include wondering how the type bias of the therapist was interacting with the type of client he or she had. Eventually, we began using the Enneagram as a way to build team unity and trust and as a means for solving staff conflicts.

At a more personal level, most members of the spiritual group to which my wife and I belonged were familiar with the Enneagram, and it became a kind of common language in our process. When I retired from full-time clinical work, I began facilitating reflective practice groups across the country for therapists who wished to bring a spiritual dimension to their clinical work. The Enneagram became a central feature of our seminars. Over the years, Alice and I also attended several retreats with an American Daoist[1] master, Michael Winn. They possessed a directness and experiential quality that seemed intuitively right to me, and my own spiritual development was deeply affected and enriched by them. But I couldn't figure out how to incorporate

1 You may sometimes see this word spelled Taoist. The reason for this is that there are two conventions for rendering Chinese into the Roman alphabet, the Wade-Giles and the Pinyin. This book uses the latter, except when quoting passages from authors who use the other convention.

Daoist body cultivation into the Enneagram work I was already doing. It seemed that the two had to relate to one another in some useful fashion, but applying the Enneagram to one's personal spiritual growth seemed more complicated than using it for developing group cohesion or as a clinical tool. I wanted something more than just a way of typing myself and the people I lived with. Seeking to understand the Enneagram in a deeper way, Alice and I enrolled in and completed the Enneagram Professional Training Program led by Helen Palmer and David Daniels. Meanwhile, I began writing this book that you have just opened.

Why another book on the Enneagram? There are already so many excellent books on your bookstore shelf that will introduce you to it, help you to determine your type, and invite you to explore your type more deeply. Some are kind of kitschy and fun, whereas others are scholarly and pedantic. Some reflect a Christian perspective, others have a slightly Buddhist or Sufi flavor, while yet others try to be psychologically mainstream and secular. Where does this one fit, and why might you want to read it? Ultimately, of course, you will have to be the judge of that, but I'll give you the short answer right up front. At first blush, the Enneagram seems a typology, a system for describing psychological types. It is a bit more complicated and sophisticated than some other systems out there, but for many people the Enneagram remains first and foremost a typology. I believe this is really unfortunate. To my mind the Enneagram does not describe nine types of personality, one of which is yours. It describes nine ways to *not* be all of who you are, one of which you have unconsciously made your own. The purpose of discovering your type is not simply to know how to better describe yourself, but to transform how you relate to both yourself and to the world around you so that you may live more freely as the person you were meant to be.

The Daoists' phrase for this process is "the transformation of things." The kind of transformation they are talking about is not a makeover of the physical world. For the Daoists, objects and events have little objective meaning in the first place. A situation's meaning is determined mainly by the observer's relationship to it. Thus a situation's meaning can change as one shifts how one relates to it. This shift makes it possible to spontaneously find the adaptive path in any given situation, without effort or coercion. Zhuangzi, a Daoist sage from the fourth century BCE, poetically called living like this "wandering at ease in the cage." His phrase suggested the title of this book. The cage can be just about anything: the country you live in, a terrible boss, your marriage, the state of your health or wealth, your personality, your body, or your mind. Daoism doesn't have much interest in leaving any part of the present world behind. It does not seek the Absolute in some nirvana or heaven. It simply wants to learn how to live freely in the world at hand. Nor does it care much for understanding "absolute" truths, of which it remains consistently and thoroughly suspicious. It doesn't want to know *about* but to know *how*. In this book, I want to bring Daoism's pragmatism to the Enneagram. I don't want just to tell you what your type is but how to grow spiritually within its parameters.

A second small advantage of this book may result from the fact that I spent my professional life as a clinical psychologist specializing in the developmental problems of infancy. Studying infants gives you a fascinating, different view of humanity. At least, it does this once you give up the notion that babies don't know anything and can't do very much. We used to think of them as blank slates upon which the environment wrote a life. The past fifty years of research has shown us that they are from the start far more active, aware, and "human" than we suspected. And how does this help us to use the Enneagram more effectively for our own development? The short answer (the long-winded ones you will wade through later on) is that the infant we once were is in many ways closer to our true self than the adult person we have become. Much of our true self was left behind in our hurry to grow up and join the race. The Enneagram is a kind of map, showing us how to get back there once again, this time with all of our adult smarts included. Daoism understood this in its own way, even though it had very little interest in child development, a much later western contribution to culture. Many statues of Daoist immortals show a fat, smiling old man dancing while carrying an infant. The infant holds the key to his joyful appearance, for unlike adults, the infant is open to and trusting of a presence it does not attempt to define or control.

Introduction

The fact that you are reading this tells me that you might be somewhat familiar with the Enneagram and are curious about how it relates to Daoist practice. A second possibility is that you are a student of the Dao and are wondering what its relationship could be to this system of personality types called the Enneagram (for those who skipped the Preface, pronounced EN-ee-a-gram). I do not imagine many readers will be familiar with both, which poses a small problem about how to organize this book. So right up front, I want to make it clear to those of you who are new to the Enneagram that this is not an introductory text. I am not going to start with a set of questions that will yield a score that reveals your type. Although the wish to discover one's type right at the beginning is certainly understandable, the quick road is not always the most helpful one in spiritual work. If you are unfamiliar with the Enneagram, and do not yet know what your type is, you should expect to feel slightly confused as you begin reading this book.

If you find really must end the suspense about what your type is, you can always pick up a small but priceless book by David Daniels called *The Essential Enneagram*. You can find it in most bookstores at a reasonable price, or you can probably pick up a used copy online for less than five dollars. Or visit www.enneagramworldwide.com and take the short online test. Either of these will help you discover your probable type and introduce you to its main features.

In the meantime you might simply go along with the design of this book, which is somewhat circular, spiraling back to several focal questions again and again, each time with more depth and precision. And if you are already quite familiar with the Enneagram, be prepared for a new approach that sometimes looks at things in a different way from the one you are accustomed to.

If you are new to Daoism, don't worry. This is not a philosophical treatise, and my purpose is neither to dazzle you nor to burden you with its subtleties. Nor is my purpose to instruct you in advanced levels of Daoist practice, for that I am not capable of doing. My purpose is simply to approach the Enneagram from a Daoist perspective.

Daoism is first and foremost a practical method for spiritual growth. Its origins are quite simple. The first known use of the term *dao* in classical Chinese literature is as a verb form meaning "to change the course of a great river by digging a small trench in just the right place." Even after centuries of development, it remains a practical wisdom with a major emphasis on knowing *how* rather than knowing *about*. This practical emphasis is what I hope to impart. Whatever concepts you need in order to understand the Daoist perspective will be introduced as needed.

Even though this is not a beginning text, every book has to begin somewhere. So let us begin by asking, "What is the Enneagram?" At its most basic level, it is a system that describes nine personality types. It is a good system. I have been a practicing clinical psychologist for nearly forty years, and I have not seen a better one. Personality type is made up of two basic components: content and structure. Content refers to the unique traits of personality that can be described. For example, we can say a certain personality is tense/relaxed, optimistic/pessimistic, or action-oriented/thinking-oriented. All of these "descriptors" refer to content, and the Enneagram does a wonderfully complete job of filling in the content for each of the nine types. The second component of personality has to do with structure. Structure is what makes the content show up the way it does. For example, each personality has its own way of paying attention to what happens. This structural feature greatly determines what contents end up in the final description of the personality. If someone habitually pays attention to the negative aspect of events, his or her focus will be on threats, problems, and worries and we would end up describing the personality as pessimistic. If someone habitually pays attention to the positive aspect of events they will find support, possibilities for success, and things about which to be enthusiastic which will lead us to describe them as optimistic. In both cases, the person's manner of paying attention has an impact upon the characteristics of their personality.

Another major difference between content and structure is that we are more easily aware of content. We more or less know whether or not we feel threatened or supported. But most people are almost completely unaware of the process by which they place attention on this or that aspect of a situation. In fact, most people don't even believe that such a process exists; they think they simply perceive the situation as it presents itself. When another person sees the same situation differently, they are likely to think there is something wrong with the other person. The Enneagram is supremely good at uncovering underlying structures such as how we pay attention, what motivates us, and what we believe about ourselves and the world.

Content is either conscious or unconscious, whereas structure is nearly always unconscious. Much of the content is conscious. For example, I can tell you my name, where I was born, what my family of origin was like, my occupation, my children's and grandchildren's names and ages, what I like and don't like to do. I can even tell you with fair accuracy whether I am outgoing or shy, a risk-taker or cautious, detail oriented or big picture, etc. The parts of content that are unconscious usually have to do with painful, traumatic past events. In order to survive such events, human beings repress, distort, or deny either the events or their feelings about them. Most traditional psychotherapies are concerned with helping people discover, accept, and integrate these unconscious aspects of personality content.

The structural component of personality is usually almost completely unconscious, at least at the beginning of personal development or spiritual work. People who are basically mistrustful and suspicious of others generally don't know they are. They simply think others are not trustworthy. Many depth psychologies try to help people uncover these more deeply hidden structural aspects of their personality. The Enneagram can be tremendously useful for both kinds of work.

Is there any part of us that is beyond personality? All spiritual traditions answer this question with a resounding yes, though modern empirical psychology and the therapeutic techniques it has spawned are pretty silent on the subject. A helpful way to distinguish the personality from what lies beyond it is to think of personality as the "me" and the other dimension as the "I." The "me" is the sum of all of one's psychological content along with the structures that give rise to it. Most spiritual traditions call this the ego. (Daoists call it the *xin* or heart-mind.) Beyond the "me" or ego is "I"—awareness, pure and simple. Awareness is said to be formless because it has no content and no structure. It is presence—that presence to oneself without which nothing else can be present. There is only one such awareness because presence is utterly simple and cannot be divided into parts. The presence in you is identical to the presence in me, for we are both "I" in equal fashion to ourselves even though we each possess a distinctly different "me". "I" can never be known in the usual meaning of the word "to know." It is not a content that can be described, and if I try to do so, whatever description I come up with simply gets shoved into the "me." Trying to know *about* "I" is a little like trying to step on the head of your shadow. It keeps moving just ahead as you as stick out your foot to capture it.

All spiritual traditions—Christian, Hindu, Buddhist, and Native American, to name a few—place the attainment of the "I" experience near the center of their spiritual practice, although they have different names for it and different understandings of what makes it possible. Daoism is no exception. In fact, Daoism is one of human history's most thorough attempts to move beyond conceptual knowing to direct awareness.

Daoists call conceptual knowledge based upon principles and abstractions *zhi. Zhi* gives you a perch, a place from which to appreciate. But you always have to remember that tomorrow a better foothold may appear, and if you want to ascend the mountain, you must be ready to relinquish the foothold you already have for the next one higher up.

Direct awareness, on the other hand, provides a concrete sense of a person or thing—its particular uniqueness at the moment it presents itself. If *zhi* is knowledge of the mountain's weather patterns and topology, direct awareness (called *wu zhi* or formless knowing) is your underlying sense of being conscious and fully alive as you get to know "this mountain, this day" firsthand during the climb. *Wu zhi* is always "so," for it is always rooted in just this moment and just this situation. The personality or "me" is not capable of achieving this kind of awareness. It can only be had from the point of view of "I." Once achieved, however, such awareness makes possible "effortless action" (called *wu wei*), which is action that springs forth without premeditation and is in precise accord with the necessities of the concrete situation.

This may all sound rather confusing at first but you may be getting an initial idea of how Daoist practice is geared to transcending content and form and reaching a deeper level of experience in which one's thoughts, feelings, and actions arise naturally, without effort or resistance, and in turn create harmony rather than conflict with the environment. I want this book to take your study of the Enneagram to that deeper level. At its most basic level, the Enneagram is a map of the ego. It is a very good map, probably the best ever devised. Once you have the map, however, there is more to do than just memorize it. If you want to reach a new and more profound level of spiritual experience, you need to begin exploring the described territory for yourself.

Since I have just called the Enneagram a map, it probably makes sense to give you a map of where we are going. Imagine the map in the shape of a tree. We will travel up the tree, starting at the bottom. Part I, the Roots describes two underlying components of the structure of personality or type: the ways we sort and process experience and the fundamental kinds of energy we use in the process. A basic familiarity with these two components will help you to reach a deeper awareness of your individual way of experiencing life and the aspect of life energy that you primarily rely on as you do so. The whole purpose of reading Part I is to ask yourself, which of these ways of experiencing life is my own, and which of these energies is the one I most often use? Your answers will provide you with an elementary basis for recognizing your own type as well as that of others. Part II, the Trunk, begins by explaining the function type plays in daily life. It also tells you how to recognize when type is getting active or going on automatic pilot. Lastly, it gives you some preliminary ideas about what to do when that happens. Part III, the Canopy, takes each type in detail, laying out each type's native manner of expressing original nature or essence and its initial wounding and subsequent development. Following a description of how each type develops is a section on the path of healing for each type—the type's point of avoidance, its vice and virtue, and the place where they begin transforming one into the other, called the Pivot of Dao. As each type is presented, the Pivot of Dao notion will become clearer, so that by the time all nine types have been discussed you will have a fairly complete idea of how to access it for yourself. Part IV of the book is called the Cosmic Tree. The first chapter of this part looks at the Enneagram as an archetype of the human condition, and the second describes four basic principles of spiritual work regardless of type.

In the appendices, you will find concrete suggestions on how to begin or to enrich your meditation practice, a brief history of the Enneagram, a theoretical examination of how the Pivot of Dao leads to self-transformation, and a short annotated bibliography of books about the Enneagram.

PART I: THE ROOTS

The Developmental Structure of Type

We begin by looking at two deep structural components of personality or type. These operate almost entirely outside of conscious awareness. They were formed early in development, during infancy. One has to do with the basic filter we use in order to process experience: visceral, emotional or mental. The second is the aspect of life energy we most often rely on: *yin*, *yang*, or reconciling.

Chapter 1:

Three Fundamental Ways to Process Experience

Brief Introduction to the Enneagram

The term Enneagram is derived from the Greek words *enneas* meaning nine and *gramma* meaning writing. Hence Ennea-gram means a "nine-writing." Its origins go back some six thousand years to Sumer (present day Iraq and Iran) where it seems to have been introduced to describe fundamental laws of the development of everything—from the cosmos itself to your newest baby nephew. It was generally drawn as a circle in which are inscribed an equilateral triangle and an irregular hexagon:

Figure 1:
The Enneagram Symbol

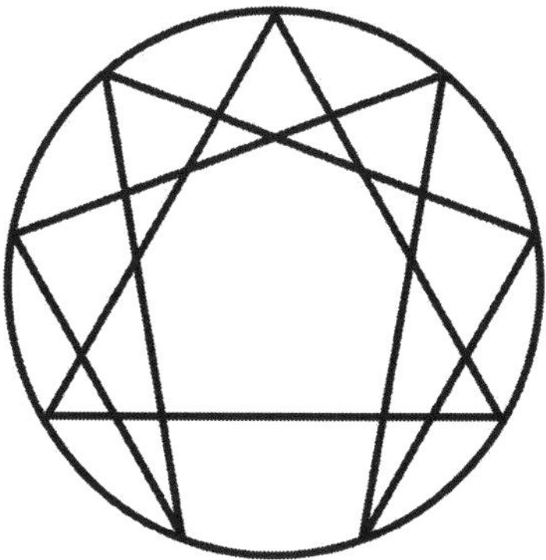

In modern times, the Enneagram refers to a system that describes nine personality types (or nine versions of "me"). For those who are unfamiliar with the system, each type is identified by a numeral and sometimes by an additional word or two of description. The descriptive words change slightly from teacher to teacher but the numerals do not. The types may be briefly described as follows:

1. Ones: Perfectionists
   These are conscientious, dependable people who bring clarity and order to life. However, their belief that there is only one way to do things correctly can make them rigid and intolerant.

2. Twos: Givers
   These people are sensitive, caring, and warmhearted, but they so intensely enjoy helping others that they often end up trying to do for others what others could better do for themselves.

3. Threes: Performers
   These are highly motivated, effective people to whom success seems to come naturally. However their focus on achievement often comes at the cost of inner feelings and relationships.

4. Fours: Romantics
   These are emotionally intense, creative people who seek deep connection with others. However, their inner feelings of being alone and misunderstood can be over-dramatized in ways that end up pushing others away.

5. Fives: Observers
   These folks are analytical and self-sufficient. However, their fear of being overwhelmed by the demands of others leads them to withdraw and safeguard time and energy for self.

6. Sixes: Loyal Skeptics
   These people are imaginative and perceptive and often have a pleasingly offbeat sense of humor. However, their tendency to focus on potential dangers and others' shortcomings to the exclusion of everything else can turn them into a burden or even source of conflict to others.

7. Sevens: Epicures
   These are energetic, buoyant people who bring fun and endless possibilities to family and friends. However, they can be self-

centered and so inclined to escape boredom and pain through distraction that others find them unreliable.

8. Eights: Protectors
   These are strong, direct people who are concerned with justice and fair play. However, their all-or-nothing style often seems overbearing to others and can be exhausting to themselves.

9. Nines: Mediators
   These are salt of the earth people who will give you the shirt off their back. They are calm and able to see all sides of an issue but often find it hard to get going and make decisions when they are needed.

The Three Centers of Experience

The Enneagram divides these nine types into three major groupings called triads.

Each triad contains three types who share the same predominant way of processing experience. One group processes experience viscerally in the belly, a second group emotionally in the heart, and the last group mentally in the head. The distribution of types and triads around the nine pointed symbol is given in Figure 2.

Figure 2:
The Distribution of Types and Triads

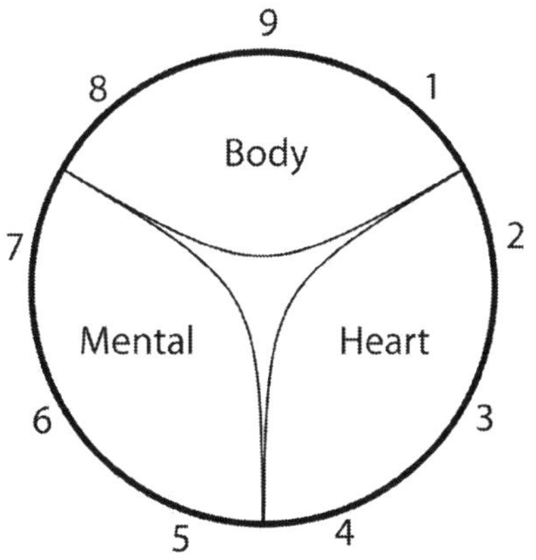

Daoists call these three centers *dan tian,* or fields of elixir, locating the lower one just below the navel and a few centimeters inward, the middle one at the level of the heart, and the upper *dan tian* between and slightly behind the eyes. The idea of three centers may at first seem strange to some readers, but it is quite common to most ancient traditions. And it probably should not come as a surprise to anyone with even rudimentary knowledge of neurology, for it nicely mirrors the modern division of the brain into hindbrain and stem, mid-cortex and limbic system, and neo-cortex and pre-frontal lobe. In evolutionary terms, the hindbrain and stem are the oldest sections of the brain. Often referred to as the reptilian brain, they deal with basic functions like breathing, temperature regulation, hunger, and sex. The limbic system and mid-cortex are more recent developments. Called the mammalian brain, they regulate feelings and emotional bonding. The newest additions are the neo-cortex and the pre-frontal lobe. Primarily hominid elaborations, they allow for planning, foresight, and abstract thinking.

The older world traditions did not reduce all of these functions to a brain located in the head, but divided them between the belly, the heart, and the head. (Actually, modern neurology would also tell us that the brain is not located solely in the head but is distributed throughout the body.)

The body, heart, and head centers are often referred to today in Enneagram circles as the three centers of intelligence. In this book, I prefer to call them the three centers of experience, because I think the word intelligence suffers from our western bias toward conceptual rather than energetic categories. Daoists would be unlikely to use the term centers of intelligence because they believe the central task of self-transformation is managing energy rather than mastering concepts. Daoist practice is not so much concerned with discovering universal truth but with maintaining harmony with life's natural movement. Accordingly, the three centers are looked upon as fields whose function is to receive and circulate three different types of the life force, which is called *qi* (sometimes written *chi* or *ch'i*).

Body Center

The body center (sometimes referred to as the belly center) operates viscerally, through sensations and instincts. In the Daoist view, the body center is the seat of *jing qi*, or vital quintessence. Vital quintessence is life energy in its purest and most rarified form, caught as it were in the act of transitioning from the non-manifest world to the manifest one. Frequently in these pages, I will suggest that the human soul can be regarded as a Being-Loving-Aware. That is, the soul can be thought of as the part of us that simply wants to be "here," welcoming into awareness the miracle of life that is happening at this very moment. The body center is the home of the Being aspect of the soul, or the aspect that seeks simply to be "present". It is the center we most often rely upon when our very existence is being threatened. *Jing qi,* therefore, is concerned with three basic functions: survival as an animal, power necessary to function within the animal hierarchy (matriarchy or patriarchy), and sexuality in its aspect of procreation.[2] The awareness of the body center, therefore, is attuned to the physical energy of others and to the life force itself. The conscious aspect of body-centered experience is its quality of presence, sensed as immediacy ("there," "just so"). Its higher manifestations in consciousness are the feeling of being grounded and solid and of the discernment of power needed to act in a given situation. Its lower manifestation is an underlying sense of anger and resentment about how the physical world impinges upon the self with all of its demands and necessities.

If you are a body type, you may have some difficulty recognizing that this is your predominant center of experience. After all, you grew up in a culture that is radically alienated from the body and rather ignorant of its manner of knowing. Quite possibly when you were small, you may have frequently encountered occasions of being sure that you "knew" the truth of some incident but had difficulty putting your felt sense of the event into words. Because you experienced life primarily in the body, it took you a few moments to move your experience up from the belly to the head and to translate your felt sense of a situation

2 For those readers already well versed in the Enneagram, these three aspects correspond in turn to the Enneagram's three subtypes: self-preservation, social, and one-to-one.

into concepts so that you could communicate it to others. You knew what you knew, directly and without words. But at school and perhaps even at home, the preferred way to communicate one's experience was verbal, and your visceral way of knowing may not have been given sufficient recognition and encouragement. As a result, you may have felt slightly inferior. This feeling may have led you to neglect your body experience and move everything up into the head since that made you seem more like everybody else. Take a few moments therefore to ask yourself where you first "know" something. For example, when you meet someone, where do you first "get" what kind of person they are? When you enter a room full of people, how do you first know what is going on? When you react to some circumstance, where does the reaction begin? If you are a body type, you will recognize that you don't do these things by thinking in your head but by sensing in your body.

The belly center of experience's chief characteristic in consciousness is the utter certainty with which it senses whatever it perceives. When you know something in the body, it seems beyond all doubt. This sense of utter certainty is a tremendous advantage when your very survival is threatened, for at such a moment the last thing you want to do is to sit down and weigh alternatives. However, there is a downside, too. As we have all experienced on occasion, gut instinct can sometimes be dead wrong!

Heart Center

The heart center perceives through emotional pathways. The heart center of experience is concerned with the personal aspect of the life force, or human *qi*. Human *qi* is the energy we use to construct and maintain a sense of community with all living beings and is related to the aspect of soul I call Loving. Much of its activity lies below the level of explicit consciousness. The heart center is sensitive to the moods and feelings of others and to one's own perceived worth in their eyes. It endows what it knows with personhood, life, and value. Unlike mental perception that creates distance between knower and known, emotional knowing enhances connection between them. Just like vital quintessence, human *qi* also serves the three functions of survival, social and one-to-one relationships. The emotional/recognition system by which babies and parents bond and become attached to one another provides a survival function for the infant. The affectional/belonging system of human tribal identification guides the child to become a member of the social group. Finally, the emotional/erotic ties of pair bonding provide people with the motivation needed to achieve intimacy with a partner.

If you are a heart type, you experience life primarily in and through your feelings. You don't have to go looking for them or figure them out through a process of reasoning—they just appear in your consciousness. You also read other people's feelings easily. More importantly, you *want* to connect to others on a feeling level. This search for connection is your greatest strength for it makes you compassionate and open-hearted. The disadvantage is that the urge to remain constantly connected to others can dull your inner sense of self, making it necessary for you to find yourself in and through the reactions of others. This can make you vulnerable to fluctuations in your sense of self worth caused by other people's reactions, comments, and moods.

Head Center

The head center connects to the world through thinking. The aspect of soul to which it is especially attuned is the Aware function. Although the head center is the home of analytic and logical thinking, Daoists see it as more than just a generator of ideas. The higher *dan tian* is also home to what is called the numinous mind, which is the foundation for mystical experience. The energy of the head center is called *shen* (spirit or numinous). *Shen* has three functions. It performs a survival function, for without *shen* even the physical organs of the body forget how to function and die. It performs a social function in that it grounds the perception that all beings are one. Finally, it provides the energy that connects each individual to the Source, which would seem to be the ultimate one-on-one.

If you are a head type, your everyday awareness feels like a conversation in the head. You have a sense that "you" are somewhere inside your thoughts, which seem to reside in your head. You spend most of your waking moments thinking, which feels like talking to yourself. It is hard for you to not think. The great advantage of this is that you are good at predicting and managing events. The big disadvantage is that the mind is also a generator of fear, doubt, and mistrust, for the mind can dispute anything it conceives. This is especially likely when thinking is cut off from the energy of the heart and the belly.

If you do not yet know which center is the one you most depend on to process experience, start observing yourself. It may be helpful to focus on times when you meet something new—greeting a stranger, entering a meeting at work, or taking your first walk around a strange city. Conversely, you might observe your reactions during a routine and familiar experience such as driving to work or dining with family or friends. Where does your experience begin? Does it start with the sensations in your body, the feelings in your heart, or the thoughts in your head? If you want, ask a friend or someone you live with. How does that person see you? The process of self-observation or of asking for feedback from others will do you good even if you fail at first to come up with a definitive answer.

How the Centers of Experience Develop

Do infants already experience life primarily through one of these three different centers? It is difficult to say with any certainty. Infants show significantly distinct temperamental styles even in the neonatal ward. Yet the tri-partite division of brain functioning in the newborn is not yet clearly differentiated, for the infant's brain is still busy organizing itself for many months after birth. What accounts for the fact that adults end up with one dominant center of experience? And most important, what do the three centers have to do with the central spiritual task of reclaiming our essential nature as expressions of the one fundamental consciousness or "I"? In the two sections that follow, you will find a brief description of how infants seem to experience the world, followed by three early childhood experiences called *shocks of embodiment* that change their experience. For me, the transition tells a story of how our original state of innocence is transformed during early childhood into something else that we now call "normal" life. My hope is that the short digression will better equip you to ponder how you became your particular personality type, how it continues to function, and to what extent the automatic nature of its functioning causes you suffering.

Three Elements of Infantile Experience

We can begin by describing the three elements of infant experience, elements that can easily be observed during the first two years of life but that are often overlooked or misunderstood. I call them Presence, Joy, and Awareness of Others' Awareness.

Presence

The first element is the quality of Presence. Because it appears in experience prior to any thought or concept, Presence cannot be defined in words. It is that presence to oneself without which nothing else could be present. It is pure awareness—bare of all internal commentaries, judgments, comparisons, fears, or desires. Such is the awareness I observe in a calmly alert newborn, whose tiny body sometimes seems reduced to just a pair of eyes totally absorbed in sights that are still fresh, unlabeled, and unburdened by the weight of prior experience. I am tempted to say that such an infant is not only present, but that he is an embodiment of presence itself.

A calm, alert newborn is present in this manner because he has no other choice. His experience is of necessity devoid of memories of previous similar experiences, expectations of what this new experience should or should not be like, or desires of wanting it to end or to go on. The infant, without knowing it, is simply present to the miracle of being.

The adult has largely lost this capacity because he or she is so wrapped up in internal commentaries about this moment being interesting or boring, good or awful, about how well or how badly one is handling it, about what went on last night, or about what one is going to do next. All of this *thinking* makes it impossible to be utterly, simply, and without distraction present to the moment. Indeed, we are so accustomed to living like this that we rarely notice that anything is wrong. Sometimes, when the internal voices grow raucous, attacking us or attacking our loved ones, when the boredom grows so intense we cannot bear to wait for tomorrow, or when the hopelessness lies so heavily upon us that we can no longer even contemplate tomorrow, then we know something is wrong. When the absence of Presence grows this intense, we call it a disease, give it a diagnosis, and offer a treatment. The duller, more daily lack we simply call Life. Perhaps that calmly alert newborn is inviting us to challenge this complacency.

Joy

The second element of infant experience is Joy. Joy is the natural consequence of Presence. It is the experience of feeling opened up and drawn toward something or someone with a strong sense of wonder, curiosity, and interest, in the absence of any fear or feelings of rejection. I think you can see its beginnings at least by three months in the face of an infant greeting her mother. It seems even stronger by five months when you can witness a baby using his shining eyes almost like another pair of hands to keep from falling over as he tries to grasp a brightly colored toy. It is undeniable in the fourteen month old bestowing his Dalai Lama smile from his supermarket cart on each and every passerby.

In adult life, this sense of Joy is often noticeably lacking. The immediacy and openness of being fully drawn toward whatever experience is at hand is rarely felt by us. In its place, we have accepted a somewhat duller substitute, which we call "feeling happy." Even this we usually experience either as a memory of some past pleasure or as a daydream of some future one. In fact, many of us would think it weird to meet a person who was simply happy to "be here." What would you really think if a colleague came into your office and whispered, "Isn't it wonderful simply to be here this morning?" We seem to believe that that kind of joy is suitable only for small children. Even our best theories of development are remarkably silent about its loss over time.

Awareness of Others' Awareness

The third element is Awareness of Others' Awareness. This is the realization that we all share the experience of being present. It is the intuition that I am not alone, that there are other centers of conscious experience out there, and that they are very much like my own in that they sense, feel, and think just like I do. This ability is often touted to be the crowning achievement of human development, the psychological tour de force that sets us apart from all other species. A fair amount of attention is devoted to it in the developmental literature. Those who do research on infants can observe its rudimentary presence in the facial resonances of a four month old and his mother shown on split screen TV. They are quick to point out that these synchronies of shared emotion will soon develop into the capacity for shared attention, or the baby's capacity to notice what his mother is paying attention to and thus to divert his own attention to that same event or thing. I remember once as a student watching shared attention blossom for a little girl I was observing. Ever since she had been born her mother routinely sang a little ditty to her. By seven months, she had learned to wave her arms as her mother sang. Beginning at her seventh month of life, the little girl introduced a new twist. Immediately her mother stopped singing the little girl stopped moving her arms. Two weeks later, I watched her introduce a fascinating variation to the game. She stopped waving her arms five seconds after her mother's song got underway. Her mother obliged her by falling silent in mid-syllable. The little girl would grin, wait, and then wave her arms again like a choir director to make her mother begin singing. Five seconds later, she would stop waving and laugh when mommy once more stopped singing.

This awareness that "you-are-also-aware-as-I-am" seems to commonly sprout forth at about eight or nine months. It is accompanied by a burst of purposeful, communicative signaling by the baby, and a strong parental sense that "she has become a person!" Its full flowering will be achieved with the advent of symbolic communication and the beginnings of syntax and language over the following year and a half.

From shared affect to shared attention to shared understanding, the development of the awareness of others' awareness is a crowning human achievement. It is nothing less than the birthing of a mind. Of the three elements of infant experience I am describing to you, this is the only one western psychology has extensively investigated. Yet even so, many theories pay little attention to the manner in which this wonderful achievement is routinely diverted into something not so wonderful. The fact is that for much of our adult life we don't experience this awareness of others' awareness as a joyful sharing of the miracle of consciousness. Instead, we routinely undergo it as a rather painful set of internalized preoccupations with what others think of us, want from us, might do to us, or what we think about them or need from them. Most of the time we accept this state of affairs as normal.

I think that babies are meant to show us that we should not be so blasé about our adult experience. I think that if they could talk, they might ask us to challenge some of our ideas of what "normal" is. After all, why are babies born? On the biological level, the reason is fairly clear. They are born because cellular life is genetically programmed to senescence and needs periodic re-freshening. What is the parallel reason on the psychological level? What are babies supposed to re-freshen within the human spirit? I suggest that it has to do with Presence and Joy and Awareness of Others' Awareness. If so, a complete theory of human development cannot uncritically assume that the mental life of the infant is simply a state of deficiency waiting to be remedied. Even less so can it assume that the remedy is the set of cognitive and emotional skills that enable the infant to become efficient but hassled adults just like us. Such a theory needs to pay more attention to the ongoing tasks of adult life. In particular, it needs to pay more attention to what infants can tell us about what we have all lost during childhood and what we can do about recovering it.

I do not mean by this we should over-romanticize infancy. The infant experiences Presence without even knowing that he is doing so. The infant's Joy at being here quickly dissolves into disorganized panic if others fail to provide his basic necessities or to hold him gently in their minds. His Awareness of Others' Awareness does not allow him to take the other's point of view, or even to realize that there *are* points of view. The infant is not yet reflectively aware of himself. The development of a coherent sense of self is a major task of childhood. I simply want to emphasize that in the usual process of developing that self, something precious is routinely lost. Let us take a closer look at what and how. It may help us begin to understand that the loss does not need to be permanent.

The Three Shocks of Embodiment

The appearance of each newborn brings tears of joy, not just to parents, but even to nurses and doctors who witness the event day after day. Why is this experience so powerful? I believe its power originates in the mystery of our own arrival. The human soul has three functions: to be present, to be joyful, and to share the single point of awareness that grounds all existence. As we have just seen, these functions are very much alive upon our arrival. The healthy baby of an unmedicated mother is born alert and fairly calm. He manages to wiggle up his mother's belly to her breast if allowed to do so. And if misfortune or modern medicine prevents him from having this experience at birth, he will usually get another chance soon.

You and I had some such passage into embodied consciousness. We had no language with which to encode it, so we cannot remember it in story form, but we experienced it nonetheless. Our first experience of being present as a body filled us with awe, and it happened in the company of at least one other human being. I believe it is the lost joy of that moment that brings the tears to our eyes at the sight of yet another arrival. We still long for the purity of that first moment of simply loving being here together, for we are at our deepest soul level a Being-Loving-Aware. Whenever we encounter other such moments—in nature, in romantic love, with our children, friends, teachers, and therapists—we inscribe them in our memories as signposts to guide us back to similar encounters again. This is our nature. In the spiritual traditions, these are called sacred spaces, encounters with Essence or *yuan qi*, the original life energy. We had our first taste of them, if we were fortunate, as we arrived.

But we could not maintain the experience. As newborns we were not always calm and alert. In fact, we usually spent only minutes in this state before cycling toward states of sleepiness or distress. The taste of original life energy was real, but apparently we were not meant to hold it on our tongues forever. The fullness of *yuan qi* appears to be a core or root energy of human existence, but it seems the nature of roots to remain subterranean. If subjected to perpetual daylight, they soon die. And so once embodied, we quickly began to experience other aspects of being human, some of them harsh and demanding. Inevitably, these experiences began to limit our openness to being fully present, joyful, and aware. The spiritual traditions sometimes refer to these experiences as the three shocks of embodiment. I call them Loss of Wholeness, Loss of Emotional Connection, and Loss of Trust. As we shall see, they seem to have something to do with both the development and the maintenance of our Enneatype.

Loss of Wholeness

The first shock is a result of physicality itself. We have little idea currently about how the shock of physicality is experienced in the womb, but we have some idea of what happens during and shortly after birth. Immediately we leave the security of our mother's body we begin to discover that existence as a physical organism is difficult. In our modern world, only a minority of newborns get to crawl slowly up their mother's belly to the breast. Instead, they are suctioned, wiped, weighed, and examined. Even under optimal conditions, the arrival is soon found to be rather complicated. Exiting the weightless conditions of the womb, babies find themselves thrust into a world of gravity. It takes effort to move. Their skin, accustomed to the unchanging liquid environment of the womb, now encounters things that are hard or rough, hot or cold. Additionally, they must regulate body temperature, breathing, heart rate, and daily sleeping and waking cycles. They must learn how to take in milk, swallow it, digest it, and eliminate its by-products. They must also learn to regulate the amount of sensory stimulation they take in through their senses. The realization of just how difficult it is to be in a body is the first step in the loss of full access to original life energy with its willingness to be fully open to every experience.

Embodiment also entails living in a physical world full of discrete beings distributed in space and time. Babies' gradual realization that they are living as separate individuals in such a world gradually engenders a sense of lost wholeness. Their original feeling of being "one with" is lost, and they are left to deal with the hardships of feeling separate and alone. Gradually, their ability to remain fully present is obscured. They are no longer able to be simply and completely open to all experience. Some of it is just too painful. Those infants whose discomfort reaches overwhelming levels can develop a chronic sense that being a body involves a more or less constant sense of both pain and feeling separate. The lost sense of wholeness tends to generate a dull, visceral, and often unconscious sense of anger about being an individual center of consciousness tied to a physical body. As we shall see later on, that anger can become the emotional engine that runs certain types of egos.

Loss of Emotional Connection

The second shock is the loss of connection. It is the infant's gradual realization that his or her emotional ties to a caregiver do not always bring pleasure and joy. Modern infant studies have elegantly described the infant's original readiness to form a deep and permanent emotional connection to caregivers. The technical term for this process is "attachment."[3] It is quite possibly the most important learning process of one's entire life, and it all takes place before one has language. Simply put, each baby is born with a heart wide open, ready to make a deep and lasting commitment to its caregiver. This deep connection is in a way a buffer against the first shock of embodiment. It softens the blow of being in a physical body. But it brings its own hardships as well. Deep emotional pleasure cannot always be maintained in human relationships. The natural ebb and flow of emotional connectedness

---

3 This readiness is our evolutionary heritage, developed over hundreds of thousands of years as our ancestors began to walk upright on their two hind legs. The human pelvis became ever slimmer, making walking easier and more graceful. But as the pelvis was narrowing, the size of the newborn's skull was simultaneously increasing. That put the female body on a collision course with the prospect of ever more difficult and dangerous childbirth. Biologists invented a fancy word for nature's eventual solution to this problem; the word they coined is *neoteny*. Neoteny is the process of giving birth earlier and earlier to ever smaller and more premature infants. Human newborns, because of their greater prematurity, are more deeply and lastingly dependent upon caregivers for their survival than the newborns of any other related species. Human caregivers in turn must devote far more attention and energy to their babies. This requires an immediate yet lasting surge of emotional intensity in the parents' hearts, an intensity that is to a large extent ignited by the infant's own readiness to initiate, engage in, and maintain an emotional relationship.

over time can leave an infant with an occasional sense of being unseen and unimportant. Repeated exposure to such experiences can produce a basic belief that one is fundamentally invisible and unlovable. Gradually, the capacity to remain fully open to emotional experience closes down the baby's original capacity for joy. Just as loss of wholeness produces anger, the loss of connectedness closes down the infant's capacity to experience joy. For some children it begins a lifelong effort to make themselves more visible and lovable. That effort often serves as a second basic kind of emotional engine for ego development.

Loss of Trust

One of the most important, distinguishing characteristics of each baby's original energy is receptivity to others. Infants instinctively trust in the presence of as yet unknown persons who will be mindful of them. This capacity, so crucial to the flourishing of the spiritual life, is once again an evolutionary heritage. Babies come into the world ready to make a connection to whomever is there. They do not demand references or credentials from their caregivers. They arrive ready to trust, ready to share their bodies, hearts, and eventually their very awareness with them. But over time, real life challenges that trust. Babies discover that people can just pick them up and put them down where they please. Or that they can shut them away and forget about them. They come to recognize and perhaps even to expect their caregivers' failure to provide a perfectly secure holding environment. Even the best intentioned and best prepared parents are sometimes unavailable. With some regularity, they can misjudge or simply not notice their infant's needs. And unpredictable, overly intrusive, withholding, depressed, or angry parents can so deeply traumatize some babies that they become chronically fearful and mistrustful of the very people on whom they most depend. In such cases, they develop an unspoken but pervasive belief that their original state of trust was simply too dangerous to maintain. As a result, fear and mistrust become yet a third source of emotional energy for the developing ego.

The gradual loss of trust in the outside world also has an internal effect. Babies do not at first recognize themselves as separate psychological beings. They are like supremely good dancers who move with their partner as though they were one being. Their feelings, like their patterns of attention, tend to move in synchrony with those of their caregivers. In the beginning, infant consciousness is experienced as shared awareness or the intuition that all awareness is the same. It is the conscious awareness characteristic of "I." But by the second half of the first year of life, this awareness is submerged by a powerful new form of consciousness. Babies learn that they are psychologically separate from their parents. They become aware that they can have their own feelings and can pay attention to something even though no one else is paying attention to it. As their consciousness gradually separates out into a state in which self and other are sensed as distinct, any developing mistrust of others also starts to extend inward toward the child's own self. He begins to mistrust his own capacity to influence others and produce desired results. Not only does the environment seem dangerous, but the child's ability to influence it seems too weak and inefficient. Eventually, the child loses confidence in his or her ability to reconnect to the original state of presence, joy, and shared awareness. With this, the loss of original energy becomes complete. Loss of wholeness, emotional connection, and trust ultimately entail loss of the ability to be present and joyful in shared awareness. What is left is an ego struggling to survive in a world that seems alternately yet unpredictably comfortable and harsh, loving and lonely, trustworthy and downright dangerous.

The Three Shocks, Centers of Awareness, and Enneatype

Do these three shocks somehow influence the way small children develop a preference to depend upon one center of experience more than upon the others? All children presumably experience all three shocks, but not all seem to experience them to the same degree. Are those most affected by the shock of lost wholeness likely to become body types, those most hurt by the shock of lost emotional connection predisposed to become heart types, and those most traumatized by the shock of lost trust inclined toward mental types? Or does the causality perhaps work the other way around, a native predisposition toward a particular center making the infant more prone to a certain shock? The question, like all nature-nurture questions, is intriguing but not always very enlightening. Its answer will lie at the level of knowledge *about*—

useful, interesting, perhaps necessary to seek, but only a placeholder until a more complete theory arrives.

However the causal interaction between the three shocks and the three centers of experience is conceptualized, the cumulative effect of the three shocks upon the child's ability to remain open to the full flow of life energy is a gradual loss of presence and the emergence of reactivity and loss of harmony. A person's actual connection to original energy cannot ever be lost. (If it were, one would simply cease to exist.) But awareness of the connection can be lost, and as it is lost, a blockage of energy occurs. The blockage acts like a kink in a hose. Or to use an example from living things, when a tree's life energy is diverted outward toward a new branch a mark forms within the fiber of the wood at the place where the original energy changed course. We call the mark a knothole. Something similar happens in developing children's consciousness. As awareness of original essence is lost, life energy is constricted, forming a kind of psychic knothole. A pattern of reactions crystallizes like a protective shell around this knothole. The shell is the ego. All egos, regardless of their eventual type, are basically the same. They are the result of the soul's identification with form as it loses sight of its nature as formless consciousness. That is to say, the infant gradually becomes convinced by the shocks of embodiment that he or she is this body with these feelings and these thoughts and that he or she is *only* this. It is this identification—I am a "me" and only a "me"—that ultimately makes us feel separate, alone, and lost.

According to the Enneagram, one of the ego's major illusions is the belief that it can undo the effects of this loss of original wholeness. The ego wants to regain the lost fullness, but since it does not remember how it lost it in the first place, it can only do so through its own striving and thus can never succeed. It is forced to create a facsimile, a false copy of the lost quality. The full blown container of this facsimile is called an Enneatype. One of its basic patterns is a tendency to experience events either viscerally, emotionally, or mentally. Regardless of which tendency we have, our Enneatype veils our awareness of original energy, prompts us to seek it elsewhere, and thus prevents us from accessing its power. No matter how knowledgeable, how skillful, or how well adjusted our personality is, it is fundamentally a mark of lost connection to the only energy that can bring us true peace and happiness. It keeps trying to find alternative sources of energy, peace, and joy, but it cannot, and this is why no matter how much we learn, how successful we are, or how many friends we have we continue to suffer. The ego may have helped us survive the pain and traumas of childhood and get on with life's journey, but it can never carry us home.

The constriction of each individual ego has effects upon the whole human community, and indeed the entire world. Daoists believe that all living beings are sustained by one field of *qi*, the breath of the original life force. Any limit placed upon the natural flow of life force within one part of a field to some degree restricts that flow within all other parts. The constriction of each ego thus serves to constrict all others. Our collective maintenance of this constriction is called "the obscuring of *Dao.*" Hindus call it *maya*. Buddhists call it *samsara*. Christians name it *original sin*.

Chapter 2:

Three Fundamental Aspects of Life Energy

Yin, Yang, and Reconciling Energy

Most spiritual traditions recognize three manifest forms of life energy. Usually they are called the passive, the active, and the preserving forces and are sometimes represented by a trinity of gods, for instance Brahma, Shiva, and Vishnu. I will be using the Chinese version of this trinity, which has several distinctive features. Classical Chinese cosmology recognizes only one primordial energy, called *wu qi*, which is formless. (The Hindu tradition calls the formless source of everything Atman, which like *qi* is imagined as a breath. A similar notion appears in the Bible's opening description of creation, in which the "breath" of God is said to move silently over the formless deep. Each tradition has its own story of creation, but the underlying imagery remains the same.) For Daoists, when primordial energy becomes manifest as the world of forms, it is said to possess two fundamental aspects, *yin* and *yang*. These two aspects in turn have a relationship to each other and that relationship introduces a third element into the equation, that of balance or harmony. In this book, I am calling that third element the "reconciling" aspect of the life force. In Daoist teaching, the relationship between *yin* and *yang* is represented as a circle divided into two fields by an S-shaped line. One field is colored blue and the other red. Blue symbolizes water or *yin* energy while red stands for *yang* or fire energy. (See Figure 3.) Each field contains a small dot of the opposite color. The dot of opposite color reminds us that all *yin* energy contains a *yang* aspect, and that all *yang* energy is partly *yin*. The circle printed on a page is stationary of course, but the idea is that *yin* and *yang* are constantly revolving and giving birth to one another. The constant balance of their movement constitutes the reconciling aspect. All three elements together represent *Dao*, or the eternal process of the formless giving rise to form.

Figure 3:
The Symbol of Dao

A Cautionary Distinction

In order to avoid needless confusion for readers familiar with the Enneagram from other books, I want to distinguish these three aspects of original energy from a conceptual scheme often found in traditional Enneagram teaching. I am referring to notions of moving toward, moving away, and moving against, first formulated by Karen Horney[4], an early psychoanalyst. According to Horney, the ego can either "move away" from psychic pain by going unconscious and numbing out, "move against" the pain by opposing it and trying to eradicate it, or "move toward" the pain by trying to incorporate it and use it as a lever to accomplish something. At least two major schools of Enneagram teaching have adopted this terminology into their understanding of the distinctive styles that each of the nine personality employ when dealing with interpersonal relationships. Don Richard Riso and Russ Hudson propose that three of the nine types (Four, Five, and Nine) withdraw or "move away" from social contact, three others (Three, Seven, and Eight) assert themselves or "move against" social contact, and the last three types (One, Two, and Six) comply or "move toward" social contact. Helen Palmer also applies Horney's categories to interpersonal

4 She wrote before the Enneagram was introduced to the United States and had no knowledge of it.

styles but comes up with a different grouping of types. She describes types Five, Six, and Seven as moving away, types Two, Three, and Four as moving toward and types, and Eight, Nine, and One as moving against. However one chooses to make these distinctions, it is important to remember that Horney's three categories have nothing to do with Daoist notions of *yin*, *yang*, or reconciling energy. These latter have to do, not with defensive movements or interpersonal styles, but with fundamental qualities of the life force itself. Any attempt to reduce them to Horney's three categories is only likely to cause confusion.

Yin

Yin is absorbing energy. It is sometimes called the passive force, although this can be misleading. *Yin* energy falls, settles, and condenses. It is receptive and therefore is often called feminine, but one has to be careful here. Femininity is but one example of *yin*, for *yin*/*yang* is a far more basic distinction than even female/male. To reduce *yin* to a feminine, open, and receptive interpersonal style is to limit its scope too narrowly. *Yin* energy absorbs, but is not always ladylike, for it sometimes absorbs in order to annihilate. *Yin* is such a fundamental quality that it can hardly be defined in a simple sentence. As we shall repeatedly observe, the classical Chinese worldview is not logical/analytic but associative/poetic. The best way to understand a notion such as *yin* is to become familiar with a wide range of its usages.

So we can say that *yin* is the energy of the valley. A valley is the space where the mountain no longer is, since it has worn away. The power of *yin* energy stems from its quality of absence. It is the energy of a hollow or emptiness. This quality of emptiness may at first make *yin* energy seem fragile. After all, it simply accepts whatever comes to it. So our first impression of a valley overwhelmed by spring floods might be that it has been vanquished. Yet the truth of the situation is that the floods will soon recede, and when they do, the valley will remain. Indeed, it will be even more *yin* since now it will be deeper.

Or to use a very different simile, *yin* energy is like that of water. It takes the shape of whatever contains it, which may make it seem rather passive. Yet like water, *yin*'s still depths exert tremendous pressure and can crush whatever they incorporate. Finally, we must remember that *yin* energy, although still, is never static. By its very nature, it is the beginning of *yang* (recall the red dot in the center of the blue field). To revisit the two metaphors used above, a valley that has been inundated possesses enormous fertility to create new life. And water that seems so easily pushed by wind or pulled by sun and moon can be so powerful that it wears away even the hardest granite shore.

Yang

Yang energy expands, rises, and evaporates. It is often called the active force and is associated with the masculine, but again one must be cautious not to make a simplistic equation. *Yang* is the energy of the mountain. It is created in fire just as mountains are created by volcanoes. It reaches upward and outward, changing, creating, and destroying. At first glance, *yang* energy seems bigger than *yin*. We North Americans have a tendency to think that all power is *yang*. We are quite taken with the fact that *yang* energy is capable of producing elemental changes. Have you ever seen how a blast furnace transforms iron ore into steel? It is a spectacular sight. Yet the fire that seems so powerful is actually quite evanescent compared to the steel. The eruption of a volcano is extraordinarily violent, yet it is over in a few days whereas the mountains last for millennia. The crashing of ocean surf puts on a spectacular display of force, yet the ocean which contains the wave endures undisturbed. Ultimately, *yang* energy is no more powerful than *yin*. It is simply the beginning of *yin* (the blue dot in the red field). The mountains created in fire contain springs which are the source of water that flows down to first make and then irrigate the valleys. In the ultimate analysis, *yin* and *yang* are wholly complementary, each requiring the other to achieve its ends.

Reconciling

Finally, the traditions often speak of a reconciling or preserving force. The Chinese do not call it a "force," for strictly speaking, it is not a distinct form of energy but the relationship between *yin* and *yang*. Its function is to seek a balance between them. Its presence nevertheless has energetic effects and functions. Consider for instance a child's top that is spinning on a table. It wobbles from side to side, but there is an unmoving balance point around which the wobble is contained by harmonizing centrifugal and centripetal forces. The Chinese call this balance point the *daoshu* or pivot of Dao. It is the hole or stillpoint at the center of the cartwheel, without which the wheel could not turn. We will have much more to say of this in later chapters when we consider how to transform the "fixated" energies of each type into freer versions of original life energy.

Distinguishing Among Energies

It is not always easy to tell whether a given event or phenomenon is *yin* or *yang*. That is because the two always co-exist. They only appear separate once one has adopted a certain point of view. Consider the sun and the moon. Which is *yin* and which is *yang*? If we turn to subtropical cultures such as the Mediterranean, we find that the moon is considered feminine (*la luna, la lune*). By contrast, the sun is masculine (*el sol, il sole, le soleil*). The reason seems fairly clear. In the tropics, the moon is constantly changing, waxing and waning in rhythm with a woman's cycle of fertility. The sun, on the other hand, is relatively constant just like male sexuality. But if we move northward toward higher latitudes, we find that the sun becomes the feminine element and the moon masculine. The German language for instance assigns the feminine gender to the sun (*die Sohne*) while considering the moon masculine (*der Mond*). This is because the sun is more obviously variable in the northern latitudes, changing throughout the year, whereas the moon seems relatively constant.

To further illustrate the subtlety required to distinguish *yin* from *yang*, one can ask whether anger is *yin* or *yang*. A simplistic view might argue that anger is a masculine or *yang* energy, but Daoist five-element theory actually distinguishes five types of anger, two of which are *yin*, two of which are *yang*, and one of which is reconciling! The major *yang* form of anger is rage. Associated with the fire element, it is red and passionate and wants to destroy its object by transforming it. The lesser *yang* form of anger is annoyance or irritation. It is caused by the experience of having one's action blocked and is associated with the wood element. Like a growing tree, it seeks to bend or work around its obstacle. The major *yin* form of anger is hatred. Associated with the water element, it is black and cold, seeking to annihilate the object of anger within its depths. The lesser form of *yin* anger is called stubbornness. Related to the metal element it tends to condense, harden, and turn passively aggressive. Finally, the reconciling form of anger is criticism and judgment. It is related to the earth element and attempts to clamp down on its object, put boundaries around it to limit it. So we can say that no emotion or thing or event can be definitively labeled *yin* or *yang* without considering point of view. Everything depends upon context, as one would expect from a contextual system like Daoism.

Unbalanced or "Stuck" Energy

Yang, *yin*, and reconciling are of themselves value neutral. No one is better or worse than the other. The infant's original energy (called *yuan qi*) is a perfect balance of *yin* and *yang*, pulsing in a harmonious flow. Chapter 55 of the *Daodejing* says:

> One who is vital in character
> Can be compared with a newborn baby.
> Wasps and scorpions will not sting a baby,
> Snakes and vipers will not bite him,
> And birds of prey and ferocious beasts will not snatch him up.
> Though his bones are soft and his sinews supple
> His grip is firm.
> As yet oblivious to the copulation of male and female
> His member still stands erect:
> Such is the height of potency.

Unless otherwise noted, all translations of the *Daodejing* are from Ames & Hall, 2003.

We in the west are accustomed to thinking of babies as fragile and unable to take care of themselves. And in many ways, of course, we are right. Yet we forget how marvelously in tune they are with their own life energy. The cellular intelligence of their tiny bodies produces the most intense and complicated growth of the human life cycle—all without thought or effort! Healthy babies charm their parents into falling in love without any need to plan or strategize. And when stimulation gets to be too much for the baby's nervous system to process, the baby simply falls asleep—all without effort. The flow of energy just happens, and happens almost always in accord with the infant's basic needs. As life goes on, however, the natural flow of original energy tightens up, and the balance of *yin* and *yang* is lost. The loss of balance shows up as a tendency to overuse or to get "stuck" in one aspect of energy to the exclusion of the other. A child develops conditioned patterns, automatic habits, and routines. Some of these patterns tend to be mired in *yin*-like passivity, others gush into *yang* action for its own sake, while other patterns become rigid schemes to avoid any extreme of *yin* or *yang* whatsoever. As time goes on, one form becomes dominant. Thus we find adults whose personality is unbalanced toward *yin*. They have a hard time being decisive or fending off the emotions or demands of others. Other people are unbalanced toward *yang*. They act for the sake of action, they cannot turn off their spinning minds, or they charge ahead regardless of the needs of the situation or the safety of others. Yet a third group of people become so preoccupied with balance that they actually lose their balance. They become like small children who have decided that the spinning top shall not wobble any more and put their finger on it, thus preventing it from moving at all.

Of course, no human being completely lacks either *yin* or *yang* energy. But most people tend to use one more than the other and can therefore be described as *yin*, *yang*, or reconciling types. As a practical matter, it is a good idea to become familiar with one's own tendencies in this regard, as well as with the tendencies of one's friends and intimates. The reason for this is that the energy itself becomes a kind of clue that one has fallen into the grip of one's egoic identifications. I will have much more to say about this later on. For now, here are some basic behavioral clues you can watch for. If you find it hard to see them in yourself, you may want to ask some people who know you quite well which aspect of energy they find most common to you.

Yin energy feels soft and somewhat quiet. People whose energy is mostly *yin* seem to invite others into their space. Their eyes tend to make a soft and welcoming contact. They seem to exude a sense that they present no reason to fear, that they offer a safe and quiet haven. When we meet someone who is basically *yin*, we feel a lack of edge and aggression. Because of this we may feel drawn toward them. On the other hand, we might feel that it will take some effort to contact them since there doesn't seem to be much energy reaching out toward us. *Yin* personalities usually have rounded, soft body language. They seem to fold into their chair if they are seated, and when standing or walking, they seem to be enclosed by the space they inhabit rather than to protrude out from it. Their hand gestures tend to circle back toward themselves. Their sentences often have a soft rise as the end. In some *yin* types, the energy shows up as a soft, resting energy, and our reaction to it is sometimes experienced as an urge to shake them just a little bit in order to get them going. In other types, the same energy can manifest itself as vulnerability, or perhaps a soft edge of sadness just under the surface. In yet other *yin* types, the energy seems to shrink down inside the body, and the person may seem to be protecting some precious but fragile treasure within. With all *yin* types, our basic reaction is generally one of either being drawn toward them, or a feeling that we have to use a fair amount of our own energy in order to make contact.

Yang personality types possess an energy that moves out into space. They have a presence that is usually unmistakable. Our first reaction to them may be to shrink back just slightly since their energy seems so high. Their eyes seem to be peering out, searching for contact. Their gestures tend to be pointed and moving out from their bodies. Their sentences often have a decided emphasis or "stop" at the end. Depending upon our own energy type we may feel initially taken aback by them, or perhaps relieved that we have finally met someone who is up to our own level of energy. In some types, *yang* energy shows up as power. These people seem to occupy more space than their actual physical size demands. Their voices demand to be heard (unlike *yin* types whom we sometimes strain to hear). Their opinions are given with a lot of weight behind them. They seem somehow larger than life. Other types with high *yang* energy generally show it as eagerness, optimism, confidence, and self-assurance. Our reaction to them (again, depending upon our own energy type) may be to feel slightly tired or perhaps even overwhelmed by the sheer intensity of their effort, enthusiasm, and determination to keep everything up, alive, and interesting.

Reconciling types are often the hardest to recognize. They seem to neither invite nor overwhelm. In fact, a good clue that one is interacting with a reconciling type is the feeling that one is having trouble getting a read on the other person's energy. Reconciling types have a certain quality of self-containment, at times bordering on self-concealment. This happens because they are trying so hard not to let the energy cat out of the bag. Their eyes neither reach out nor invite in; they observe without being observed. Hand movements tend to be balanced, along with the voice. The body is generally restrained just a bit. Below the surface there may be indications of underlying tension and effort being spent to keep everything under control. Some reconciling types seem physically rigid and stiff. Others seem a bit anxious about relationships or hypervigilant and habitually nervous about their own or others' welfare. The common theme for all reconciling types is preoccupation. This preoccupation can make them seem a bit narrow, and in turn can make others feel slightly uneasy in their presence without realizing exactly why.

Interaction of the Three Energies and the Three Centers of Experience

In the previous chapter, I described three centers of experience: body, heart, and head. In this chapter, I have been talking about three forms of manifest energy: *yin*, *yang*, and reconciling. How are the two sets of three related to one another? A central hypothesis of this book is that the three centers of experience and the three forms of energy interact to form the nine personality types of the Enneagram. My evidence for such an hypothesis will have to wait until we examine each type in detail later on, but in order to prepare you for where we are headed, let me outline how the interaction works. You will recall from Figure 2 that each center of experience forms a triad of three types. I am proposing that within each of these triads there is one type whose energy is constricted primarily toward *yin*, a second whose energy is constricted primarily toward *yang*, and a third whose energy is primarily limited to reconciling. Figure 4 details where each form of energy shows up in each of the three triads.

Figure 4:
Interaction of Centers of Experience with Forms of Energy

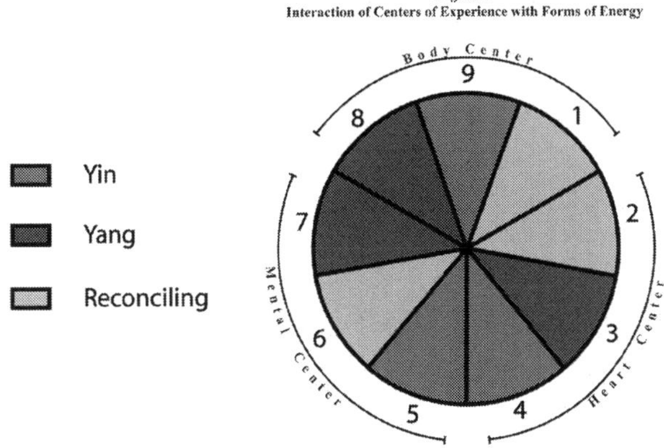

An important corollary to this hypothesis is that by knowing which center of experience and which form of energy is primary for you, you can determine your type. Suppose that you recognize yourself as a person whose energy is primarily *yin*. If you also know that you primarily process your experience conceptually through your mind, then there is a very good chance that you are a type Five. If you do so through your body, you are likely a type Nine. If you do so through feelings you are probably a type Four. The same process can be used for those who recognize themselves as primarily *yang* or reconciling. If you feel fairly sure of both your energy type and your preferred center of experience, you should be able to recognize your type. As you become more familiar with recognizing energy styles and centers of experience in others, you can use the same process to identify their likely types.

The Roots of Enneatype

We have been talking about the roots of Enneatype, the basic forms of energy and manners of processing it that result in one type or another. But what is the root of our individual being? And if we were to discover it, to find a word for it, would it remain the root as such, or would it become, like an exhumed specimen, something antecedent that is no longer a living root? The intuition of an extraordinarily important foundational stratum lying just beyond ordinary perception is remarkably constant throughout human history. People have always sensed that there is something more to consciousness than that which can be grasped by ordinary perception, something more important, more lasting and real. That is to say, people have always known that there is more to them than just their personality. But having sensed this possibility, people have always run into the maddening impossibility of giving this "something more" any persuasive definition. Billions of words have been spent trying to define its ultimate significance, and we still cannot name it in any satisfactory fashion. Nonetheless, we keep trying, for we keep catching glimpses of it. Many observers have felt that infancy is a time when humans regularly have such experiences. And so there has been a persistent notion throughout the ages that infants are in touch with some pristine quality of being, some secret vision of the ultimate mystery that is forgotten as they move forward into adulthood.

The Enneagram offers us a map that can help lead us to reclaim the pristine quality of our original life energy. Like Daoism it seeks to retrieve an original state of wholeness in which we are simply "present" without resistance to the miracle of being unfolding within and around us. The "roots of Enneatype" is a phrase that can ultimately be understood on many levels. It can refer to the content of an explanation such as, "This is how I came to be my type." Daoists call this kind of conceptual language *zhi*. It is a conceptual platform from which to examine and communicate. It is useful, but one must never forget that a better one may appear tomorrow. The hypothesis I just introduced, namely that *yin*, *yang*, and reconciling energies interact with mental, emotional, and body centers of awareness to generate the nine personality types of the Enneagram, falls into this category. It's a nice idea perhaps and offers a simple way to understand why there are nine and only nine types. You will form your own opinion of it as you read further in this book. Hopefully, you will find it useful. But it will only go so far in helping you to live more freely. Ideas about energy are not in the same league with practices that change energy. The merit of my hypothesis, if any, is that it focuses on energy and the management of it and not on the traits or contents of the "me" or the story each of us carries in our head about the past. The story only locks one into a certain viewpoint about what it means to be a certain type. What I need in order to change my life lies not in the past but in the here and now. More than a new story, I need a new way to manage my energy. For example, as a type Six, I can support my spiritual growth if I remind myself of the following: "I notice fear arising whenever I experience an impulse to trust, so let me just be still when that happens in order to let myself fully savor the experience, and then we'll see what becomes of that impulse and its energy." That will get me a lot further in my spiritual journey than endlessly repeating, "People like me are afraid to trust because our parents were so unpredictable."

Understood in this way, the roots of Enneatype designate a deep stratum of unexamined sensations, feelings, and beliefs that not only nourish the behavior of Enneatype but invite us to recover the power of our entire soul, as well. Roots lie buried from view. If you dig them up in order to study them, they soon cease to function as roots and change into something quite different. If you want to know them *as they are,* you have to be willing to let them remain hidden, their presence known only through their effects and their quality of seeming non-present. Roots belong to the earth. Not earth as in dirt, but earth as in ground. Earth is a dark energy. It is hidden, moist, and feminine. The roots of identity that lie buried in it operate mostly outside of consciousness, and for this reason they can often seem troublesome. Many of us want to weed them out and throw them into the compost. In my experience, this simply does not work.

At its deepest level, the phrase "roots of Enneatype" refers to the sacred energy within us that is the very ground of our being. That energy may have become unbalanced and stunted during our childhood but simply hacking at it will, in fact, harm us. Instead, we need to find some way to access its full manner of being, to enter its darkness, and to drink its still subterranean waters, which alone fulfill.

PART II: THE TRUNK

The Self-Maintaining Nature of Type

In the following chapter, we will take a small but important step toward gaining freedom to roam freely within our type as we describe how type manifests itself in daily life, what it feels like to "bump into" our type in action, and what we can do to begin liberating ourselves from its automatic grip.

Chapter 3:

Enneatype as Protector of the Ego

The trunk is designed to protect, preserve, and support the living tree. From the outside, it is hard and firm, unchanging with the seasons and resistant to pressures to bend in new directions. Yet on the inside, it is a busy, mostly liquid environment, perpetually in motion. It constantly mediates food and energy between the roots and the foliage. Your Enneatype is like a trunk. It supports and preserves your egoic existence as this particular "me." It is resistant to change; you will find it difficult to design new fruits and flowers for it to produce. But it also contains hidden energies from deep within that you very much need in order to reconnect to your essential roots. So it is not a good idea to try to demolish your Enneatype. In this chapter, we will take a look at the first tasks of spiritual development once you begin to incorporate the Enneagram into your practice. Let us begin with what type "feels like."

First of all, there is a big difference between *knowing* my type and *feeling* it leap into action. To know my type, I only have to learn and remember a number. "I am a Six. I know that because it was one of the high numbers on the test I took, the people interviewed on the Six panel seemed the most like me, and my teacher thought it was a good fit." I can know my type without really understanding anything more. But to feel my type going into action is much more complicated. It involves looking for something called your passion, which at the beginning of the search is more or less completely unconscious.

The Nine Passions

Each type has a passion (sometimes called a vice). The passion is the emotional energy that drives the type. One can think of it as the felt distillation of a certain form of energy (*yin*, *yang*, or reconciling) through a certain center of experience (body, heart, or head). Since it is part of the structure rather than the content of the type, the passion usually operates outside of conscious awareness. The passions form early in childhood as babies discover that their original energy is too much for their caregivers to support and nourish. They find they must limit and clamp down on that energy so that they can stay in relationship with the adults who care for them. They do so by relying more and more on one form of life energy and one center of processing experience. The Enneagram calls the constricted versions of that original energy the nine passions. Corresponding to each passion is the type's virtue, which is the unconstricted version of the passion. In this section, we will focus on the passions. If you have read other books about the Enneagram, you already know that the nine passions are those nasty words placed at the head of the description of each Enneatype as follows:

1. anger
2. pride
3. vainglory
4. envy
5. avarice
6. fear
7. gluttony
8. lust
9. sloth

You probably recognize them as the seven deadly sins, plus two. (You may want to consult Appendix B for the story behind these names.)

Given that the names for the passions are so ancient, we need to interpret them for our modern ears if we are to find them useful. The passions are not "sins" in the sense that we were taught as children. Rather they are qualities that impede personal development and spiritual growth. (This happens to be the original definition of sin, before it was corrupted.) Anger, the passion of type One, does not mean a propensity for mayhem; it amounts to an unconscious internal stand against reality the way that it is. It manifests as an urgency to judge and to criticize, born of an unexamined belief that when the godhead created the universe, she or he somehow goofed. The passion for type

Two, pride, is the unconscious gratification created by a conviction that only I can do it, that they are all depending on me, for only I know what is needed and how to give it effectively. Vainglory, type Three's passion, is felt as a pressure to be always in action and visible in the eyes of others, grounded in an unconscious belief that my personal worth resides in what I do rather than in who I am. It creates the false conviction that I alone am the author of my life. Envy, type Four's passion, is an unconscious indulgence in the bittersweet feeling that others always have more goods, more success, more friends, and more love. It is rooted in a conviction that they *have* more than I because at some deep level they *are* something that I am not. It is often covered up by a tendency to publicly denigrate these same goods and qualities as ordinary and unimportant. Avarice, type Five's passion, is a felt need to carefully guard my time and space against the intrusions of others, based upon the unconscious belief that they will absorb my energy and leave me depleted if I let them. Fear, type Six's passion, is a deep mistrust of just about everything based on the unexamined belief that I am too weak and too unskilled to react successfully to life out of my own internal reserves. Type Seven's passion, gluttony, is a longing to savor all the pleasure that life has to offer based upon an unconscious conviction that any pain no matter how small will lead to total disaster. Lust, or Excess (it is not just about sex), the passion for type Eight, is unconscious pleasure sought in pure arousal, resulting in a tendency to overdo everything—food, sex, money, speed, work—and to always be pushing the envelope just to see how far it can travel. Finally, type Nine's passion of sloth is indulgence in unconsciousness itself, a kind of personal and spiritual sleepiness that leads to a neglect of what is most important to one's development.

As you can see, the passions do not place very high on the scale of desirable human qualities. Perceiving them in action generates sufficient self-criticism that most people avoid noticing them. This is the whole purpose of having a type. A type is simply a collection of habits that more or less guarantees that you will not consciously experience your particular passion. Whenever you engage in the habitual preoccupations of type, you will probably be spared the unpleasantness of recognizing that you are indulging in anger, pride, vainglory, envy, greed, fear, gluttony, lust, or sloth. And that feels good, which is why learning to *feel* your type in action is so hard. Perceiving it will at first make you feel worse. This is the basic reason why type is so stable throughout the lifespan. The more skillful type's activity becomes, the less you experience the passion that fuels it.

Let's make that a bit more concrete. I am a Six, and my passion is fear. If you had asked me forty years ago whether or not I was a fearful person, I would have said, "Of course not." I would have explained to you that I was a careful person, one who thought and analyzed and required evidence. Where is the fear in that? But let's make the example even more realistic. Forty years ago I might not have answered your question with any directness. As soon as you asked it, I would have wondered why you were asking me if I was afraid. What were you trying to do? And without thinking, I would have come up with an answer that changed the subject to something else. The entire response would have emerged so quickly and smoothly that the tiny moment of fear when you first asked me the question would never have appeared in my consciousness. This is how type successfully prevents a person from experiencing a passion that runs his life but which he has been avoiding for years. Type is so well practiced and so well honed that it just does its job without us needing to think about it. This is why Gurdjiev, who re-introduced the Enneagram to Europe in the early twentieth century, called type a form of falling asleep.

Perceiving Type in Action

All of this suggests that the first steps of self-transformation as you begin working with the Enneagram will be difficult. They require that you search for a sensation, feeling, and state of mind that you automatically avoid. This is totally counterintuitive. Why go looking for something that feels bad when you have already learned to escape awareness of its presence? This seems a recipe for insanity, not growth.

The reason to go looking for one's passion is that it is the emotional engine that keeps the whole egoic self looking for a false payoff. For example, the passion for type Seven is gluttony. Gluttony is the *yang* energy behind the Seven's continual need to taste a little of this, a little of that, always skittish about anything that looks slightly dull or painful. Gluttony fuels the Seven's entire mental manner of processing experience, causing the person to move like a butterfly from idea to idea, from one pleasant option to another. Gluttony is the emotional component to the Seven's mental conviction that suffering in any form, once entertained, will never go away. As long as it remains unconscious, that conviction can remain unchallenged and intact.

As you begin the work of self-transformation, you may discover that your passion is hard to find. First of all, you may not even know your type with any certainty. Actually, that is not a bad state of mind to be in. Many people quickly determine that they are this or that type only to find out several years later that they were mistaken. "Knowing" your type is really less important than "inquiring within" about the energies and processes that motivate you. If the answer does not come quickly, do not worry. The inquiry will often be far more beneficial than the answer. So begin your inquiry with a search for the underlying feeling or motivation that drives your habitual behavior. Keep the list of nine passions in the background at first and look for your own words to describe your basic motives. If one of the nine passions begins to emerge as a likely candidate, check it out with someone who knows you intimately. Don't rush to conclusions, and if you have friends who are somewhat familiar with the Enneagram, receive their suggestions gratefully but with a grain of salt. If you have a trained Enneagram teacher available, go for a consultation. But always remember this; only you can discover what motivates you. Looking for that motivation at the innermost level is an important part of the process of self-transformation. Don't shortchange yourself.

As you begin to close in on your underlying passion, you will encounter a second difficulty—unwillingness to face it squarely. Often the best clue that one is about to hit pay dirt is a kind a sinking sensation in the stomach: "Oh, not that!" If, for example, you are a Two, at first it may be humiliating to realize that you are run by a preoccupation over your own importance, hidden beneath constant attention to others' needs. Searching after your passion is truly difficult. The good results promised you are not only invisible, but at first they don't even sound worth the risk involved. So the first step in self-transformation with the Enneagram is the willingness to try something new. For many of us, this willingness comes only after we arrive at a point in life in which we realize that all our past attempts to make life manageable have failed and that we do not know what to do. This state of not knowing what else to do is often the only thing uncomfortable enough to make us willing to embark upon a path that brings immediate discomfort.

Points of Avoidance

Each type has what is called a point of avoidance. A point of avoidance is the activity or behavior the type never engages in, at least not willingly. Type One's point of avoidance is the frank and open expression of anger. Although angry inside, Ones don't like to admit it. It makes them feel that there is something terribly wrong with them. "I feel angry" is automatically transformed into "You are wrong." That way the internal experience of anger can be hidden and its open expression avoided. Twos avoid awareness and expression of personal neediness. Since their self-worth resides in doing for others, they feel deeply ashamed when they need to ask others to do something for them. When a Two feels needy, the habitual reaction is to begin taking care of someone else. Threes' point of avoidance is failure. Failure makes them feel hollow and deeply unworthy. They automatically transform little failures into partial successes—telling themselves that they almost succeeded and that now they know what to do to achieve success the next time. Fours avoid ordinariness, which causes them to experience an immense sense of shame. They seek emotional highs and lows, great ecstasy or great suffering, and avoid being in between where all of the ordinary folk hang out. Fives avoid open-ended commitments of their time, space, and emotional energies. Because they are afraid they will suddenly find themselves empty, they husband their emotional and physical resources for themselves and fill their minds with knowledge instead. Sixes avoid spontaneity. Plunging into unrehearsed action terrifies us, so we rarely take the plunge. We prefer to analyze, to think, and to live in our imaginations instead. Sevens hate all limitations, whether the limitations come from others' demands or from the perceived limitations of boredom and routine. To be limited feels excruciating, and Sevens would rather die than live that way. Eights recoil from any circumstance that makes them feel small or vulnerable. Weakness feels so shameful to them they automatically assume the power role in any potential conflict. Finally, Nines avoid the discomfort of conflict because taking a personal stand might bring about separation, leaving them to feel isolated and alone. We will have more to say about these points of avoidance in later chapters when we take up each type individually. For now it is enough to give an initial description. For your convenience I have summarized the passions and points of avoidance for each type in Table 1.

Table 1: Passions and Points of Avoidance

Type	*Passion*	*Point of Avoidance*
One	Anger	Open Anger
Two	Pride	Personal Need
Three	Vainglory	Failure
Four	Envy	Ordinary Living
Five	Avarice	Emptiness
Six	Fear	Spontaneity
Seven	Gluttony	Pain
Eight	Lust (Excess)	Vulnerability
Nine	Sloth	Conflict

The points of avoidance have practical importance because they are doorways into the passions. They are less unconscious than the passions and therefore a little easier to work with. Once engaged, however, a point of avoidance will automatically bring its associated passion into play. That is why the search for one's passion usually starts by consciously choosing to engage one's point of avoidance. Suppose you think you might be a Three. Your point of avoidance is failure. If you want to perceive your passion of vainglory, take note of your failures. Usually you immediately transform each failure into a partial success: "I almost succeeded, and now I know what to do next time in order to really succeed." Instead of doing that, just recognize that you failed *and start looking for the feeling or the physical sensation this recognition brings.* If you are a Three, you will discover is that there is a very strong expansive energy in you that wants to do whatever is necessary to change this little defeat into a partial victory. You might notice, for example, that just saying "no, thank you" to someone's request to take on a volunteer post can feel like a failure to you. As a Three, your energy is unbalanced toward *yang*. Allowing even a small defeat to resonate within you feels too passive and *yin*, and so you avoid it. The expansive energy can easily generate a stream of words in your head trying to convince you that you did win somehow, or it might present as an impulse to take a second shot at the task. It wants you to keep up your image of success so you won't have to experience any sense of failure.

Similarly, if you are an Eight, your initial task is simply to notice your aversion to feeling vulnerable and the immediate rising of that immense lusty *yang* energy that wants to make it go away. If you are a Five, your task is simply to notice how the energy to pull away and hold yourself within arises whenever a friend asks you to commit to something. As a Five, your energy is unbalanced toward *yin*. Your friend's request requires you to bring up some expansive *yang* energy and that feels so uncomfortable that you shrink from it. Finally, if you are one of the types whose energy is unbalanced toward reconciling, engaging your point of avoidance will bring up the twin discomforts of *yin* and *yang* simultaneously. Suppose you are a Six and your boss wants you to do something you know will be harmful to the project you are working on. You know you have to speak with him about it. Half of you is terrified of his potential reprisals (which makes you feel weak, which seems too *yin*). The other half of you wants to berate him for every stupid decision he has ever made (which feels far too *yang*). Your natural inclination is to waffle between both energies so that you don't have to experience either of them fully. Often the result is that you avoid the conversation with the boss, or if you do have it, you somehow manage to blow it. Your first task in Enneagram work is really not about convincing your boss or learning how to speak to him without falling apart. The first task is simply to allow yourself to feel both sides of your energy and the discomfort of being caught between them.

In summary, your first step in Enneagram work is just to notice the discomfort of allowing the unwanted energy to become conscious. If you want to experience your passion more fully, try an experiment. When you bump into your point of avoidance, rather than avoid, fight or give in to the energy that it arouses, just relax and *do nothing but observe its presence.* You are not looking to eradicate it, nor do you want to start acting it out. If you choose either of these last two alternatives, the passion will only grow stronger. The simple act of observing the passion is enough to begin the process of healing, because the one who observes is not being driven by the passion. The one who observes is closer to your true essence. Above all, remember that no matter what your type is, your first attempts to simply allow the underlying passion to arise into consciousness will cause you some discomfort, but they will not make you fall apart, go crazy, lose all your friends, or become a national laughingstock!

Befriending Your Passion: The Inner Smile

David Daniels, one of my teachers, is always telling me, "Bill, once you can see your type and feel its passion, befriend it." At first I found this counterintuitive. Who wants to be chummy with anger, pride, vainglory, envy, avarice, fear, gluttony, lust, or sloth? What does "befriend" mean here?

The ego's natural reaction to any clear expression of its passion is to judge it negatively and then attempt to get rid of it. The superego gets into high gear and begins to rant: "Did you just notice how lazy you feel? That's not how you're supposed to live your life. It's high time you do something about it!" The body tenses up; we hold our breath for a moment. And then we go into one of Horney's three classic modes of getting rid of any painful experience. The first mode is to anaesthetize the painful feeling by going unconscious. "Feeling like a failure? Get busy on another project, and you will forget all about it." A second way is to oppose the feeling. "Want to tell her off? Just smile while you bite your tongue." The third possibility is to engage the passion and use it as a lever to achieve an escape. "Feeling useless and unimportant? Find someone even needier than yourself and start taking care of them!" These are the three ordinary ways that we get rid of what we do not want—we just zone out and feel nothing, we suppress the feeling, or we somehow bend it to our own ends.

Befriending the experience is fundamentally different from any of these because it does not seek to get rid of the experience. It is based upon a compassionate and non-judgmental acceptance of a reaction that has arisen in our field of awareness. It wants neither to negate, suppress, nor magnify. It cares only to observe, the way you might observe a child who is stealing a cookie from the table. You smile to yourself because you see the whole situation—the child's wanting, the cookie's appeal, and the lack of immediate deterrence—and you realize that on the grand scale of things this piece of naughtiness is quite innocent. It requires nothing from you but acceptance. You do not need to lecture the child; nor do you need to go out and buy ice cream to go with the cookie. Can you imagine being that kind of parent—to yourself? That is what befriending your passion means.

There is a concrete practice that can help you learn to do this. It is called the Inner Smile. You can try it right now. Put your fingers to the corners of your mouth and rub them outward along the smile line. Feel your face soften. Gently place the tip of your tongue to the roof of your mouth, just behind your upper front teeth. Do it gently, don't push. Rub your fingers along the smile lines some more. Feel what happens inside your face. Can you feel your mouth soften? Now let the softness fall from your mouth down inside your chest. You can let the smile go right to your heart. Take a full breath. Feel the softness. It is both relaxed and expansive, a wonderful balance of *yin* and *yang*. Draw the next breath all the way down into the belly, under your solar plexus. Keep smiling. Let yourself feel how present, joyful, and aware you are this very moment.

This is the Inner Smile, the central practice of all forms of Daoist meditation.[5] It is simple; it is physical. It can be done at any time, any place. It has tremendous power to heal, precisely because it does not seek to change anything. It is a wonderful antidote to the Inner Frown most of us learned to practice earlier in life. Done for fifteen seconds twenty-five times a day, it will change the course of your life. I promise.

---

5 For a complete description of the practice and its ramifications, see Winn, 2003.

The Inner Smile works better than fighting experiences we don't like. Fighting requires force, and the application of force always produces an equal and opposite counterforce. Constant prohibitions *beg* us to pay attention to what is forbidden. Banning behaviors or substances simply makes them seem more attractive. As an old friend of mine used to say, "Look at the fields; see where the cattle usually stand—next to the fences!" And yet this is precisely what most of us do—we struggle against feelings and experiences we judge negatively, rarely taking the time to observe how the very struggle magnifies their importance to our lives.

For most people, the major reason that fighting with unwanted experience fails to produce results is that the fight gives energy to the story connected to the experience. For example, let us imagine a Two who is feeling rejected and unappreciated. She has been doing and doing for her child for decades, yet the child won't even call her on her birthday. The Two can try to end the experience in one of the three ways we mentioned earlier. She could simply move away from it by shifting all her energy to another person who needs her help. Or she could move against her resentment by telling herself that perseverating on it just shows how spiritually inept she is, which, of course, will only worsen the resentment. Or she could move toward it by doing even more for her ungrateful child (and all the while complaining to her husband and friends). Any one of these simply adds to the story line—the first by creating a new (seemingly better) story, the second by adding the story itself to her list of short-comings and self-judgments, and the last by re-telling the story one more time, only louder.

The Inner Smile requires no story. It focuses on the experience in the here and now. The here and now has nothing to do with the history of the Two and her child. It has to do with a physical sensation and a feeling state located within the body. Resentment is at root an energetic sensation, a tightening, sourness, or heat in the chest. Focusing only on the sensation shifts attention naturally away from the story woven around the experience and redirects it toward the experience itself. The experience is unconditioned. It is new, unstructured, and free. The story about the experience is not new; it is conditioned, practiced, and limiting.

Smiling also adds a special energy to the attention practice. It is a decision, a deliberate choice that focuses one's attention toward the physical sensations in a positive and receptive manner. It then drops down to the heart where resistance to the experience can be eased. In the past we reacted against painful experiences by tightening up. The impulse *not* to experience pain caused us to constrict somewhere in our body, and the experience became frozen there, unable to move. That frozen energy needs the heart's warmth in order to melt it.

When this occurs one is finally free to drop even further to the lower *dan tian*. Its "earth" energy is unconditioned, always new, always in the here and now. These three steps—relinquishing the "story" associated with the experience by focusing the mind on the physical sensations; smiling, thus applying the energy of the heart to the experience; and dropping all the way down into the belly center—open all three centers to the life force energy itself. This allows us to release the constriction of energy we have built up around the experience, and if done as described above, will regularly produce a sense of compassionate acceptance and calm stillness.

The Inner Smile is thus a practice that restores balance to the three centers of experience. Rather than remaining "stuck" in one center, we can begin to metabolize the stored pain and suffering that fills the ego and to release some of the constriction that keeps it intact.

So, you may well ask, if the practice is so simple and so effective, why did we not hear of it sooner? Why did we not come upon it naturally? And most importantly, why are we going to find it so hard to put into daily practice?

You did not hear of it sooner because it is counterintuitive. Relax into what hurts you? Only Lamaze birthing coaches tell expectant parents this, and even then, it sounds a bit strange. Relaxing into pain is not what a child does spontaneously. The natural response is to hold the breath, tighten the body, and shut down the window of awareness. Only when supported by someone whom the child trusts can a child relax in the presence of pain. Our deeper wounds happened when we were alone, or worse yet, they happened at the hands of our caregivers. Many of us can locate a memory that symbolizes the moment when we froze inside, blocking our original energy. In actuality, we probably experienced many such moments over and over, but you may find that one such moment stands out like an icon, holding all of those experiences in one symbolic memory.

Once the constriction happens, it becomes self repeating. The next similar painful experience is reacted to even more quickly, before it can even build up enough energy to hurt as much as the original one did. The freezing tactic becomes more automatic with time. Gradually it expands and solidifies until it has become our habitual shell. At some point we *identify* with it, that is, we come to believe that the whole complex of thoughts, feelings, and actions is "me" and that this is my total reality. This is how type veils our essential nature.

The self-repeating nature of such constrictions influences not only us but everyone around us. Our parents built the same kind of structures. They lived mostly on automatic pilot, reacting rather than remaining open. Therefore, they had no other strategy for pain to pass along to us. The repeating personal system of habits became a social system. It was how the whole world operated. We called it human nature.

The great spiritual masters knew about this constriction of life energy and how to go about releasing it. But as the living presence of the master grew dim with time and the followers became preoccupied with recruiting new members and preserving the organization, they lost sight of the teacher's central message. They complicated things, making them too cerebral or too moralistic. They created stories, conceptual schemes, and moral codes to replace direct awareness of making contact with essence. More importantly, they began to discourage individual attempts to recover essence and required their members to see a rabbi or priest instead. This universal human tendency to lose the simplicity of the master's teaching is the bane of all religions and systems of spiritual development. (Not even the Enneagram will be exempt from it.) It is a major reason you haven't heard of this method sooner.

There is another reason you couldn't find this solution before. You didn't discover the method for yourself spontaneously because you cannot use this method all alone. There is a paradox here. Only you can do it for yourself, yet you cannot do it alone. Only you can voluntarily sink into your own pain, seeking what lies below it, but like the child, you cannot do this unless you have the support of someone who can hold you while you do it. Bootstrapping simply doesn't work. So where does one find this supportive someone else? One can begin by finding a group of fellow seekers. This is the fundamental reason nuns and monks of all world traditions have banded together. You don't have to join a monastery, though. All you need is someone's living room. The non-judgmental support of others is extraordinarily helpful. Even so, it is my firm belief that in the end you will need to ask for the support of something larger than yourself or any fellow human being. I don't care what you call it. Name it the Higher Power, God, the Life Force, or the Supreme Unknown entirely as you wish. Nor do I care much how you understand it. You can grow spiritually within a Christian perspective or within a Jewish or Buddhist or secular perspective. But you must at some point turn yourself over to something higher than yourself. In my experience, there is simply no other way.

Thirdly, you will experience difficulty putting this method into practice. The first reason you already know—it is counterintuitive to relax into something painful that you already know how to avoid. It takes intention. Secondly, you won't find the payoff you were hoping to find. The Inner Smile does not do away with your passion. It is not a stream of radiation killing the cancer cells of type. In all probability you will repeatedly encounter the following cycle: you will feel your buttons being pushed and your passion aroused; you will use the Inner Smile; you will feel better—and within twenty-four hours that same button will get pushed again. Over time, you will find your passion becoming subtler and less raucous, but it will never disappear because it is yours for life. Remember type is not a disease—it is simply the structure that sustains your embodied existence. And finally, you will discover that the "feeling better" brought by the Inner Smile is not always bliss or rapture. It usually doesn't qualify as a peak experience. Mostly it is rather quiet and neutral. And that can be a disappointment if you happen to be looking for something more extravagant.

What you will discover, however, is that life will begin to change. The observer who gives an inner smile is distinct from and free of the ego's passions and types. The act of catching oneself in their grip does not always feel good, but you can console yourself with the realization that each observation strengthens the inner witness that is the doorway to consciousness itself. You will begin to experience life differently. Your friends and family will notice you have somehow changed, and they will like it. You will find that people open up more easily to you and you remain open to them with less effort. You will find greater peace within yourself. You will be ready to begin an even deeper phase of the work, one that restores balance to the three centers of experience and to the flow of *yin* and *yang* within them.

PART III: THE CANOPY

Living Freely Within Type

The next three chapters will take up each type individually, describe its original energy (called its Holy Idea), its developmental history, and the particular way it distorts the balanced flow of *yin* and *yang*. With each chapter, I will try to elaborate more fully how maintaining still attention to the type's energy, or entering what is called the Pivot of the Dao, leads to the transformation that allows a person to roam more freely within the parameters of type.

Chapter 4:

Types Nine, Three, and Six

Figure 5:
Types Nine, Three, and Six

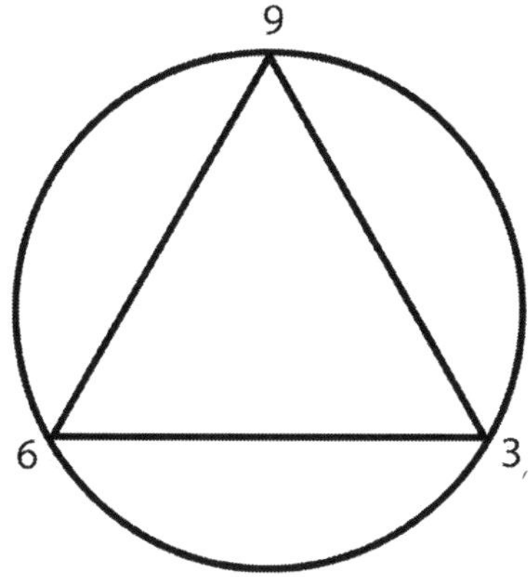

The roots of a tree contain its mysterious power to nourish and to grow. The trunk and stem exist to defend and protect the tree from wind and storm. The foliage of the canopy exchange energy with the sun and present the tree's fruits and flowers to the environment. Following this metaphor, we might say the nine types are like nine different kinds of leaves. Each has a special way of gathering the sun's energy for the benefit of the whole tree. Each also has its own set of limitations and special proneness to disease.

The Sufi tradition, which understands incarnate life as a prism that shatters divine light into many colors, teaches that each soul enters the world with a special sensitivity to one particular aspect of the brilliance of divine light. The Enneagram traditionally names nine such aspects, called the Enneagram of Holy Ideas. The term "Idea" to my mind no longer serves its original purpose, for to our modern ears it connotes something conceptual, though a Holy Idea is a spiritual intuition or awareness and not a concept. Your soul's Holy Idea, therefore, is its intuitive attunement to one particular frequency of original energy or *yuan qi*. You were born with it intact and functioning. It was not just an "idea" then, as it may be now.

This same special sensitivity, however, rendered your soul particularly susceptible to certain failures of your early environment. As described in Chapter 1, these failures fell into three major categories: loss of wholeness, loss of emotional connectedness, and loss of trust. We each experienced all three, but the special sensitivity we brought into the world may have rendered us more susceptible to one type of shock than to the others. Our reaction to that shock caused a tensing up. The tensing up created a "knot" or "hole" in our awareness. Original energy could no longer flow freely through our body. The natural pulsation of *yin* and *yang* around a balance point grew lopsided, ending in a tendency to gather excessive *yin*, excessive *yang*, or excessive effort to neutralize them both. The restriction of energy became patterned and crystallized like a protective shell around the knothole. That shell became our ego, and its particular pattern of reactivity formed our Enneatype. Hidden within that shell is what some Sufis call the "pearl without price," or our personal essence as an aware "I" who consciously realizes he or she is both human animal *and* pure conscious energy. The Enneagram is a special kind of map. It can show us where the knot is, or to put it another way, it can show us *who* we are *not*.

Having unmasked the ego, or Enneatype, the Enneagram then offers a suggestion of which direction in which to move. It tells us to start with our point of avoidance, and then suggests that we look for the energy of our type's virtue hidden within its passion. This probably sounds rather confusing, perhaps even artificial at this point. It will become much clearer as we take a closer and more detailed look at each type's path of development. For now, I simply want to provide you with a list of the Holy Ideas and Virtues for each type.

Table 2: Holy Ideas and Virtues

Type	*Holy Idea(s)*	*Virtue*
One	**Perfection**	**Perfection**
Two	**Freedom, Will**	**Humility**
Three	**Law, Harmony, Hope**	**Veracity**
Four	**Origin**	**Equanimity**
Five	**Omniscience**	**Non-Attachment**
Six	**Strength, Faith**	**Courage**
Seven	**Work, Plan, Wisdom**	**Constancy**
Eight	**Truth**	**Innocence**
Nine	**Love**	**Right Action**

We will start our exploration of the Enneagram's canopy of virtues and Holy Ideas with the three types forming the Enneagram's central triangle, types Nine, Three, and Six. Each one of them belongs to a different center of experience. Nine is a body type, Three an emotional type, and Six a mental type. Each type also constricts the flow of original energy in a different manner. The energy of Nines is unbalanced toward *yin*, that of Threes toward *yang*, and Sixes distort original energy through egoic efforts to neutralize *yin* and *yang*. The situation could be represented as follows:

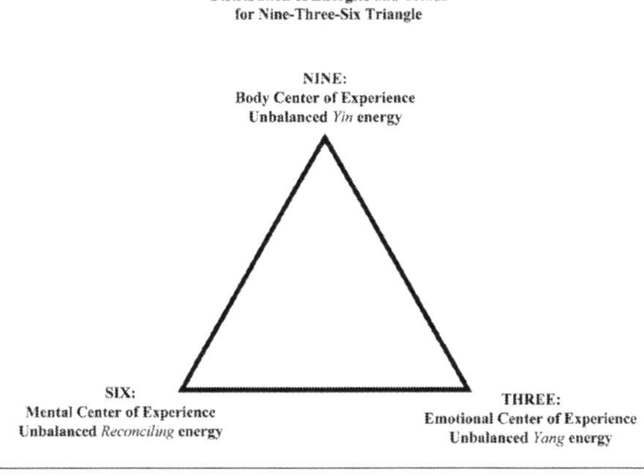

With this orientation, let us take a closer look at the Holy Idea of each Type and to what happens to it during early development. I will begin with type Nine, followed by Three, and then Six.

To those of you who are familiar with the Enneagram only as a typology, any talk about directions of movement may sound confusing at first. Recall however that the Enneagram is not simply a static description of nine boxes in which to put people. It is a guide for self-knowledge and spiritual development and that implies movement. Now while it is true that a person's Enneatype never changes, there are nevertheless important energetic shifts that happen during spiritual growth. Remember that original energy is a balanced flow of *yin* and *yang*. As the ego developed, however, the free flow of energy became unbalanced, leaning one way or the other—or tightening up into a determination to never lean at all. Spiritual growth depends to a large extent upon regaining a sense of free flow and balance, for every human being needs to have access to all three basic aspects of life energy. From the perspective of the Enneagram, re-balancing the energy of one's type entails incorporating some aspects of the energy found in the other two types which lie on the same triangle with one's own. We will have more to say about these shifting directions of movement in Chapter 7 after we describe the development of each Enneatype in detail.

TYPE NINE

Holy Idea: Love

Type Nine is the central member of the body triad. Its characteristic energy receives and absorbs, a tendency toward *yin* energy that distinguishes Enneatype Nine from the other two body types (Eight and One). According to the Sufi tradition, the Nine infant enters the world with a special sensitivity to Holy Love. Holy Love is the direct intuition of the innate loveliness of all beings. It springs immediately from the infant's openness to original energy. Love puts up no barriers. Love knows, not through images, but directly, in the body. When we see through Love, we see not with our eyes that need the light of the sun but with our hearts that perceive Being's inner radiance. Pablo

Neruda elegantly expresses this intuition in the seventeenth of the one hundred sonnets he wrote to his wife Mathilde:

> I do not love you as if you were salt-rose, or topaz,
> or an arrow of carnations the fire shoots off.
> I love you as certain dark things are to be loved,
> in secret, between the shadow and the soul.
>
> I love you as the plant that never blooms
> but carries in itself the light of hidden flowers;
> thanks to your love a certain solid fragrance,
> risen from the earth, lives darkly in my body.
>
> I love you without knowing how, or when, or from where.
> I love you straightforwardly, without complexities or pride;
> so I love you because I know no other way
> than this: where *I* does not exist, nor *you*,
> so close that your hand on my chest is my hand,
> so close that your eyes close as I fall asleep.

From 100 LOVE SONNETS: CIEN SONETOS DE AMOR by Pablo Neruda, translated by Stephen Tapscott, Copyright © Pablo Neruda 1959 and Fundacion Pablo Neruda, Copyright © 1986 by the University of Texas Press. By permission of the publisher. The Spanish text is as follows, for those who wish to peruse the original (always a good idea!)

> *No te amo como si fueras rosa de sal, topacio*
> *o flecha de claveles que propagan el fuego:*
> *te amo como se aman ciertas cosas oscuras,*
> *secretamente, entre la sombra y el alma.*
>
> *Te amo como la planta que no florece y lleva*
> *dentro de sí, escondida, la luz de aquellas flores,*
> *y gracias a tu amor vive oscuro en mi cuerpo*
> *el apretado aroma que ascendió de la tierra*
>
> *Te amo sin saber cómo, ni cuándo ni de dónde,*
> *te amo directamente sin problemas ni orgullo:*
> *así te amo porque no sé amar de otra manera,*
> *sino así de este modo en que no soy ni eres,*
> *tan cerca que tu mano sobre mi pecho es mía,*
> *tan cerca que se cierran tus ojos con mi sueño.*

St. Paul described a similar vision of Holy Love in his letter to the Corinthians (although he seems to place it in the future):

> Now we see only puzzling reflections in a mirror, but then we shall see face to face. My knowledge now is partial; then it will be whole, like God's knowledge of me. (I Corinthians 13:12)

When we are personally aware of Holy Love, we experience ourselves and all other beings as inherently, naturally beautiful and loveable since we experience everything as intimately and permanently united with one divine source. Such awareness creates a sense of being whole, completely open and peacefully at rest. We are aware of the fullness of energy within and without us. Holy Love is the ultimate ground of merger, not just psychologically but existentially.

Initial Wounding and Subsequent Development of Type Nine

Embodiment threatens such awareness. The newborn Nine registers birth and the attendant experiences of gravity's pull, the effort needed to breathe, swallow, digest and eliminate, the need to regulate temperature—in short, the energy to stay alive—as demands for more energy than is available. This is then experienced as reluctance about embodiment and difficulties with making a full commitment to "being here." One can sometimes see this pattern more clearly in a slightly older child. I knew a little boy, a Nine-in-the-making, who at the age of four was a delightfully social and engaging child. He was easy to play with because he was so willing to go along with whatever game or activity I proposed. He was so "tuned in" that he constantly warmed my heart in delight. When he played, he seemed like a comfy little body that simply went along with whatever presented itself. He was hardly ever edgy or needed to "push against" unless he was tired. When tired, he simply crashed. He left wakefulness so quickly that one got the impression he was happy to renounce it. He slept so deeply that no noise or commotion could awaken him. And when he awakened, the process was labored and slow. He whined inconsolably for a quarter of an hour or more, lost in a state of consciousness that was not quite asleep but yet defied any attempt to prod him wide awake. It was as though he was deeply resistant to full consciousness, preferring instead a dreamy state half-way between. I think of him as a still innocent exemplar of Spirit's reluctance to enter the world of Matter, doing so only if it senses the possibility of being there without being forced to face the full glare of embodied wakefulness.

When the harshness of embodied life threatens the young Nine's relaxed, open receptivity, the Nine reacts by closing in. The closing in seems to squeeze off the source of life energy. As awareness of the connection to original energy is lost, the young Nine begins to feel that the power needed to live as a separate being can no longer be found within the self. All the really necessary energy seems to reside in others. This is the start of the Nine's habit of paying attention to others while forgetting self. It begins because others still seem full of energy and power, but the self no longer does. This gives the young Nine an initial social advantage, for other people generally respond positively to the child's lack of willfulness. However, that same lack of self-promotion can make the young Nine fade into the background as the unseen member of the family. His or her sense of self can gradually feel so veiled and lost that it seems inconsequential and not quite real, and the child may begin to experience a deep sense of shame about being so utterly insignificant. He or she must then push the pain of feeling so ashamed out of consciousness. Thus the shame of being an insignificant self is anaesthetized by becoming a forgotten self. The Nine falls asleep. Sleep becomes the first and most fundamental distortion of the Nine's original absorbing *yin* energy.

But being asleep, of course, only exacerbates the sense of being lost. The ego of an unexamined adult Nine is a study in receptive energy gone awry. When it is running on automatic pilot, its habit of merging with others is so out of balance that the ego cannot tolerate any boundaries, differences, or divisions. It is compulsively passive. There is no creative juice left, for any creative act is seen as a threat to unity. The ego automatically says, "If I take any action at all, it may only make matters worse." As a result, inertia becomes a central feature of the egoic life of a Nine. (The traditional name for this is "sloth," the passion of type Nine.) This is not always immediately obvious to the Nine. Many Nines are hard workers who are constantly busy. The law of inertia however has two parts. The first half states that a body at rest tends to remain at rest. This seems to fit those Nines who have a hard time getting going in life. The second half of the law says that a body in motion tends to remain in motion. This is more typical of those busy Nines who find themselves continually occupied with secondary tasks while some important job goes neglected. The law of inertia is expressed by Nines at almost every level. They find it difficult to begin new tasks, but they also find it hard to end a task once it is begun. They learn that once they sit down to answer their e-mail messages they can easily spend the whole morning surfing the net. Experiences like that gradually make them wary of beginning *any* new task.

The inertia also extends to the mental life of Nines. They find they have trouble making choices since that means they have to change direction all on their own. They begin to depend on other people or on mere circumstance to suggest what to do next. But even then they often experience a kind of inner resistance to a suggested course of action, a resistance often heard as an inner voice saying, "It will probably take too much energy, and I won't get anything back, anyway." As a result, they find they can either spend hours doing nothing or that they can easily busy themselves with endless non-essential tasks while avoiding some decision that is central to their life. As the law of inertia plays itself out in egoic life, Nines feel increasingly stuck and paralyzed. Gradually, they begin to feel like they are cemented into some deep, unmovable, and inexpressible black hole. The hidden content of the void is anger. This unseen anger is the knothole at the center of the Nine's ego, starving it from its true source of energy.

All egos, once they are cut off from the life energy, need to create some simulation of the quality that has been lost. (This is the beautiful paradox of the ego—it is the mark of our loss of original energy yet it is also the tool we need in order to get it back.) If you are a Nine, you learned early in life to substitute niceness and comfort for Love's openness to all experience. You dedicated yourself to being affable—a nice person who made everybody comfortable. You began to follow along, avoid conflict, and compulsively behave in a kind, placid, and pleasant fashion. Of course, your attempt to recreate Holy Love by avoiding conflict was doomed to fail. Holy Love is open and receptive to all human experience, but you were avoiding one whole sector of that experience, namely anger and aggression. In the end, such a strategy of endless passivity and following along could only build resentment. Yet you had to avoid any open expression of anger because that would threaten your attempts to merge and be one with the external sources of energy you felt you needed so desperately. Your only option when angry was to get stubborn. When resentful, you got silent and withdrew. It was an inherently unworkable solution, fueled by a distorted version of your original quality of receptivity. You were trying to rekindle your original bliss by snuggling under the blankets of comfort, but when it didn't work, it seemed your only choice was to get stubborn and hide.

Point of Avoidance, Virtue, and Vice of Type Nine

The spiritual quest of type Nine is fundamental to all spiritual work. (This is why I always begin teaching the Enneagram with type Nine, for it is the fundamental fixation from which the other eight flow.) Simply put, the Nine's spiritual task is to wake up. This requires that the Nine welcome discomfort and conflict. As you know, each type possesses what is called a point of avoidance. Nine's point of avoidance is conflict, the discomfort of finding oneself in the middle of some disagreement. When running on ego power, all types simply steer clear of their point of avoidance. The individual who wants to wake up must learn to willingly enter it instead. Doing so will immediately provide an opportunity to cultivate the virtue of one's type.

For type Nine, the virtue is called right action. The term sounds a bit archaic. In its most basic sense, it means waking up to your own energy and learning to pay attention to your own internal world. This is a radical shift of consciousness away from merging with others and with the world outside the self. Your spiritual path as a Nine is to wake up and be present to your inner energy. By orienting it toward your inner life rather than exclusively to the surrounding environment, you can begin to undo the distortion of *yin* toward the sleep of self-forgetting.

In the beginning, this will feel terrifying and uncomfortable, for it will bring up feelings of personal insignificance, and buried under those you will find a wordless anger about feeling separate and alone. However, if you continue to engage your point of avoidance, to welcome situations of conflict, and, most important, to accept your reactions to them *no matter what they are,* you will gradually discover a whole new energetic dimension opening up within yourself. If you just allow yourself to feel the discomfort without needing to change, banish, improve, or manipulate it in some way, you will eventually acquire an instinctive and effortless way of reacting to conflicts and disagreements with others. It will seem that it is happening automatically, without effort on your part. Eventually, you will find that you can react to each and every situation in exactly the manner required without hesitation or effort. The Daoists call this *wu wei* or non-coercive action. The Enneagram term is right action, that is, action that moves with the situation rather than against it, which therefore creates the possibility for change and growth rather than resistance and opposition.

Pivot of Dao for Type Nine

How does this happen? The answer to this question is one of the great and joyful mysteries of the spiritual life. We do not own or control the energy needed for spiritual growth. It is there, free for the asking. It resides within the quiet willingness to simply observe, even if what we happen to be observing is our own madness boiling up once again in our heart. The consciousness that observes is not mad. It is completely sane, for it is awareness or presence itself. All one needs is willingness. For the Nine, this means the willingness to enter into the discomfort of conflict.

One of my teachers, Helen Palmer, calls this process the "vice-virtue conversion." By this she means that the basic energy of each type's vice is essentially the same energy as that of the type's virtue. In the case of the Nine, sloth is simply a constricted version of right action. The conversion of one into the other is made when one begins to "allow" the upwelling of discomfort when conflict appears rather than to "react" to it. This entails activating the inner observer, the internal witness that simply notices internal reactions without judgment, blame, or need to change them. One might schematically represent the process as represented in Figure 7.

Figure 7:
Internal Observer and Vice-Virtue Conversion

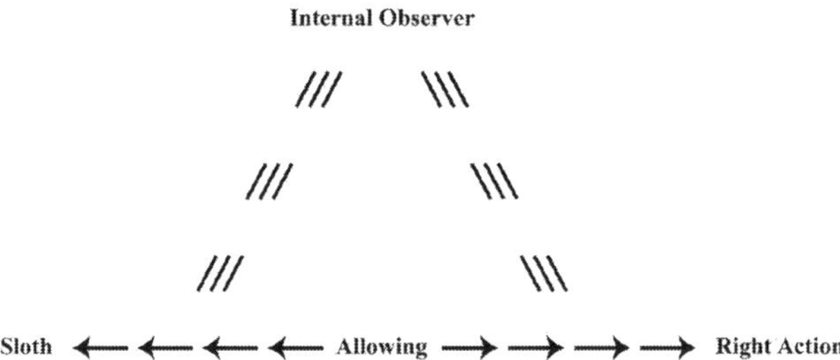

The Daoist version of this process is even more precise. Recall the symbol of Dao, two curved fields blended into a circle. One is red (*yang*) and the other blue (*yin*). In the center of each field is a dot of the other color. The dots are there to remind us that within every *yin* movement hidden *yang* energy lies and vice versa. For the Nine, willingness to undergo the extreme discomfort of conflict is the place where absorbing energy becomes expansive and passive turns active. This is, of course, hard to see when one is just beginning the work of freeing oneself from the grip of egoic life. Egoic energy—inertia, or sloth, in the case of the Nine—seems the exact opposite of right action. How does one get from one to the other?

The Daoist answer to this question is the *daoshu* or the Pivot of Dao. Daoism does not consider sloth and right action to be the opposite extremes of a two-dimensional line. It considers them instead to lie on the circumference of a rotating circle. A circle, unlike a straight line, has no beginning or end point. Imagine you held a DVD at arm's length in front of you, level with your eyes. If you hold it parallel to the ground, it will appear to be a flat line much like the diagram above. But if you rotate it a quarter turn, it shows itself to be a circle like the diagram below. So the Daoist notion of the relationship between inertia and right action is not that they are polar opposites but two related phases of the same circular energy, one phase continually giving birth to the other.

Figure 8:
Daoist View of Vice-Virtue Conversion

RIGHT ACTION

SLOTH

The Pivot of Dao is the frictionless point of non-resistance at the very center of the wheel where the seemingly opposed forces of the wheel's circumference unite. Its power resides precisely in its lack of resistance. Chapter 11 of the *Daodejing* begins: "The thirty spokes converge at one hub, but the utility of the cart is a function of the nothingness inside the hub." The nothingness (lack of resistance) at the Pivot creates the possibility of effortless action, or the knack of simply flowing toward whatever alternative best accords with circumstance. Applying this to the situation of the Nine, a still point lies at the center of inertia and action where neither dominates. Since neither dominates, each is therefore free to respond without limitation. In the pivot, there is neither sloth nor effort; there is only *wu wei* or non-coercive action.

The trick is discovering how to enter the place of frictionless non-resistance. It is easy to say, "The Nine needs to get going." But that simply opposes a *yang* force against a *yin* object. Whenever *yin* and *yang* fight, *Dao* is further obscured. Advising a Nine to "push" is to confuse right action with effort. Effort is force and force always causes counterforce. Once that happens, the *daoshu* disappears. However, if the Nine gives up all resistance even to his *unwillingness* to enter conflict, he will enter a very different psychological and spiritual space. In this space, the Nine simply allows himself to experience without negative judgment his resistance to taking action. If he does this, he will literally feel his passivity turn into an active (perhaps even angry) wish to remain immobile. This is the *daoshu*, the stillpoint wherein constricting energy begins to expand. Within this frictionless place, the Nine can slowly begin to experience the *expansive power* of his or her refusal to budge. At that point, the Nine's lop-sided *yin* energy begins to subtly include an element of *yang*. Each time this happens, the Nine can experience just a little bit more of the *yang* energy we associate with type Three. Some Enneagram teachers call this "moving toward one's heart point." Others call it "Nine moving to Three." The phrases are convenient shorthand ways of pointing to a momentous shift. But we must remember that the Nine does not become a Three. What really happens is that the Nine starts to reclaim Holy Love, which is total openness to *all* aspects of the life energy.

TYPE THREE

Holy Ideas: Law, Harmony, and Hope

Enneatype Three lies at the center of the heart triad (types Two, Three, and Four) just as type Nine stands at the center of the body triad. Unlike type Nine, however, the Three's energy is unbalanced toward excessive *yang*. When living in the automatic habits of ego, the Three's energy flows outward in all directions at once. The Enneagram tradition describes three names for type Three's Holy Idea or awareness of its original energy. They are Holy Law, Holy Harmony, and Holy Hope. The first two refer to the spiritual awareness that the life force unfolds lawfully and harmoniously in creative, unified patterns without need for any control or guidance from us. In other words, its natural flow is both lawful and harmonious with the needs of the whole. Infants with this particular sensitivity originally experience the life force as a creative energy flowing within them (more accurately, they make no distinction between themselves and the creative energy). Holy Hope is the psychological effect of being aware of Holy Law and Harmony. It is the experience of being "in the zone," creatively free and able to move without effort according to the needs of each situation. Listen to how Rabindranath Tagore describes this awareness. As you read, remember that poetry and music are identical in Bengali culture. In eastern India, you would sing and dance to this poem.

> The same stream of life that runs through my veins night and day
> runs through the world and dances in rhythmic measures.
> It is the same life that shoots in joy through the dust of the earth
> in numberless blades of grass and breaks into tumultuous waves of
> leaves and flowers.
> It is the same life that is rocked in the ocean-cradle of birth and
> of death, in ebb and flow.
> I feel my limbs are made glorious by the touch of this world of life.
> And my pride is from the life-throb of ages dancing in my blood
> this moment.

Rabindranath Tagore, *Gitanjali*, No. 69.

Initial Wounding and Subsequent Development of Type Three

The Three infant enters the world alive to the creative, living, and breathing quality of the life force. Just as the Nine enters life with a direct awareness of the innate beauty of all beings because of their interconnectedness with original energy, the Three arrives with a direct awareness of how all beings move and evolve as expressions of that energy. The energy is experienced as a field. The nature of a field is that whatever happens in one part is immediately felt in the whole. A field, even if spread out, is one unified moving organism. The infant Three intuits the life force this way more deeply than any other type. It experiences itself as a vibrant wave within the larger current of universal *Qi*. But early in childhood, the experience of being in relationship with caregivers who have themselves lost awareness of their connection to the life force threatens the young Three with the loss of this perception. That is, the Three, parented by people who can no longer themselves experience this perpetually moving, intelligent, creative facet of the life force, finds her own intuitions so unsupported that they begin to fade. Her need to remain intimately connected to her caregivers is so strong that she feels she has no choice but to allow the obscuring of *yuan q*i to happen. The obscuring is experienced as a feeling that the creative flow has faded, which leaves the Three believing that she moves and acts as a separate doer. In other words, she becomes identified with her activity. Once convinced that she is separate from the original source of life she comes to believe she herself is the cause of her activity and that her life is the effect of her own movement. The sense of being truly engaged *by and within* original energy is lost. Inevitably, the belief that "everything is up to me" brings about the death of Holy Hope. Hopelessness then becomes the knothole, which the Three experiences as inner emptiness—a sense that she is not quite genuine or real.

Threes then have to defend against the pain of hopelessness by going unconscious regarding their inner emptiness. They maintain this lack of awareness by becoming compulsive, relentless production machines. This is the primary distortion of their natural style of creative engagement. The active *yang* phase of their original energy grows so unbalanced that rather than engaging *with* the natural flow of vital essence, it engages *upon* it.

The energy of a Three living the egoic life seems to simply gush out into the world. I recall once riding in a shuttle bus to pick up my car at the airport. It was Mother's Day. The driver, an older man, asked a young, sharply dressed female passenger if she thought mothers should have to work. They immediately got into a discussion that everyone in the bus could easily overhear. In five minutes, they managed to sketch out their entire life stories, including their careers, their income levels, their marriages and even whether or not they were able to have children! Listening to them I almost immediately recognized them as likely Threes. Observing a pair of Threes running on ego power is a little like watching the two poles of that static electricity generator your high-school science teacher used to simulate lightning bolts. The voltage is really impressive, but it produces less wattage than the display would seem to imply.

Just as inertia is the prime characteristic of egoic energy for the Nine, lack of restraint is the mark of egoic energy at Three. A Three running on ego is a persistent and driven doer. (In the seventies, the California based *est* movement phrase for them was "a human doing".) The external doing is mirrored internally by the ceaseless production of plans and to-do lists. Threes are masterful multitaskers. You see them in airports, reviewing their notes for a sales meeting while chatting on cell phones with their broker as they wait in line to change seating assignments with the gate agent. While the ability to attend to many things at once is a truly great advantage in a crisis situation, the compulsion to pay attention to a variety of things at once even when things are going smoothly is simply an expression of the Three's habit of pumping energy outward in all directions at once.

Threes nevertheless feel of lot of pleasurable excitement while this energy is overflowing, and thus the excitement easily becomes a substitute for deeper feelings. It is often quite mysterious to Threes when they first hear that their Enneatype is one of the emotional types. This is because Threes often have a hard time locating and tapping into their feelings. They have learned to avoid them because they seem like a waste of time. After all, feelings tend to get in the way of accomplishing the job. People who wallow in feelings usually finish last, and the Three wants to avoid that at any cost. I once heard Eli Jaxon-Bear, an Enneagram teacher based in a Hindu tradition, say that Threes burn their feelings as fuel for all the production. I would add to this that the heat of the fire is experienced as a kind of enthusiasm, and Threes have to settle for that instead of the entire gamut of feelings.

If you recognize yourself as a Three in these pages, you probably also realize that your constant focus on *doing* requires so much psychic energy that you physically crash from time to time. This happens because "doing" is episodic. Once it is over, it is over. Nothing seems to last when all that you can experience is doing. Your energy always seems to be flowing out and away from you, and eventually you begin to feel exhausted and empty.

A further side effect of this is that Threes inevitably become preoccupied with image. Some of them are preoccupied with external image—cars, clothes, gadgets, toys, contacts, fame, power, and titles—though for many the preoccupation with image is more subtle and internal. It has to do with how useful and productive they are, how well they are accomplishing their goals. The Three's problem with image actually is a result of the illusion that who you are can only be measured by what you accomplish. Constant production makes you lose sight of your own inner constancy, and so you have to create a convincing self-image so that you can discover yourself in the effects you are producing in the world. Ultimately, you come to believe that you *are* the image. In short, you learn to manufacture the self rather than experience it as arising moment to moment within a living field of energy.

Point of Avoidance, Virtue, and Vice of Type Three

The passion or vice of the Three fixation is called vainglory. Vainglory is the constant compulsion to create one's self through action. It is the final distortion of the Three's original creative energy—the vanity of one who attempts to produce a false simulation of vital essence. Your spiritual path as a Three begins with the recognition of the compulsive nature of your need to be active.

A very good spiritual practice for a Three is to consciously decline a request to do something. Threes are so good at accomplishing things that they receive a lot of requests to take jobs, join committees, to head up this or that. If you choose to not do something, it will cause you some discomfort. (It feels like a small failure.) But if you spend even short periods of time without "doing," and if you allow yourself the initial discomfort this causes, you will begin to expose something of great importance to your development.

Your virtue (the unconstricted version of your passion) is called veracity, which means recognizing that you cannot be other than what you already are. Temporarily stopping all the doing will propel you into a face-to-face encounter with being, or with who you *are*. This encounter will gradually expose the underlying fictitiousness of ceaseless doing by showing you your real rather than produced self. This will not be easy at first, for it will immediately expose feelings of superficiality and shallowness. It will entail seeing how you can lie to yourself, how you put off and deny your internal feelings, and how you gravitate toward image. And, of course, that will bring up your point of avoidance as a Three, which is failure. You naturally shrink from failure or make some quick internal adjustment so as to redefine it as partial success. Staying with the sense of failure is hard, but it is the entry point to the *daoshu*. The frictionless pivot that allows for effortless movement starts with the Three's realization there is nothing to do but to *stop*. Stop the effort, stop the lie of authorship. Just experience the pure power of the wish to be seen as the one who can always do it, the one who always succeeds.

Pivot of Dao for Type Three

There is a marvelous teaching story about such a *daoshu* in the *Zhuangzi*, a Daoist text compiled in the fourth century **BCE.** Yen Hui is a Three-ish young monk who has set out to convert the lord of Wey, a young and ruthless ruler. He calls upon Confucius for advice. Confucius tells him he is afraid that Hui's plan is a recipe for disaster and that Wey will probably kill him. Hui insists he is only following Confucius' own advice, which is to avoid the well run states and go to the poorly managed ones. Confucius then reminds Hui that he can only impart to others what is firmly established within himself and that his scheme to overwhelm the young ruler with admiration for Hui's virtue is surely going to backfire. He tells Hui, "You are using fire to quell fire and water to quell water. That is what is called 'going from bad to worse.'" At first Hui can only offer more schemes for developing even greater virtue and holiness so as to make the willful young king see the light of Heaven. Confucius cuts him short: "Too much organizing." Finally, Hui lets himself have a small moment of defeat. "I have no more to propose," he says, "tell me the secret of it." Confucius orders him to fast, not from food but from planning. Hui is to stop listening with his ears, even to stop listening with his mind. He is to listen only to energy (*Qi*). Energy is the stillness that waits to be aroused. Hui can do nothing; only the stillness of *Dao* can succeed. Finally, Hui sees the light. He confesses to Confucius, "The whole time I was failing to get the point, it was Hui who was in charge; when I finally understood, it was not Hui who acted." And Confucius replies, "Perfect! Now you are ready to roam inside the cage of Lord Wey."

The story is a wonderful description of a Three needing to come to a point of defeat (aided in this instance by a somewhat gruff teacher) in order to stop the automatic use of *yang* against *yang* (fire to quell fire) and *yin* against *yin* (water to quell water). The point of transformation is the realization of one's foolish commitment to lifting oneself up by pulling on one's own bootstraps. Humbling to be sure but simultaneously illuminating: "I am actually being held by something else; my effort is both useless and unnecessary." When Threes start to *allow* a sentiment like that of "I give up; tell me the secret of it," their excessive *yang* energy ("Hui can do it") gradually becomes more balanced ("Hui can [i.e., 'is able to'] do nothing"). Within the stillness of the *daoshu,* the Three's anguished cry, "I cannot act" is slowly transformed into a serene "I can *not* act." The realization that one can stop making effort and that life will go on as before (often better than before) is the beginning of freedom from the fixation. It is how Threes begin to reclaim Holy Hope, the awareness that the fullness of power is already coursing through them.

TYPE SIX

Holy Ideas: Strength and Faith

Enneatype Six is the central member of the mental types. It is also what I call a reconciling type because Sixes try to "manage" the balance of *yin* and *yang* by running on automatic ego-power rather than just allowing the energy to flow naturally. The Holy Idea of type Six has two names: Holy Strength and Holy Faith. In order to understand the experience of Holy Strength, we need to rid our minds of the mostly masculine connotations the word has come to possess. Strength in this context does not refer to force or might. It is derived from the ancient understanding of the Latin term *fortitudo* (staying power) and not from its associated terms *vis* (force) or *potestas* (power). The essential quality of Holy Strength is neither *yin* nor *yang.* It is grounded in the reconciling aspect of energy that preserves and harmonizes. Holy Strength refers to the abiding awareness of the ultimate harmony between receptive Love and active Hope. It is called Strength because it remains steadfast in the face of the inevitable tension experienced once the human mind perceives original energy divided into *yin* and *yang.* From a human perspective, being is divided into active and passive, human and divine, good and evil, and so on. Holy Strength is the direct intuition of the mutual grounding of all these apparent opposites in one act of integrating presence. It remains effortlessly and unfalteringly aware that each and every event is rooted in the life force and is inseparable from it.

The psychological effect of the awareness of Holy Strength is Faith—the ineradicable sense that all being evolves according to universal love and hope. Faith is capable of holding in one unwavering gaze the world's suffering and failures, as well as its glorious evolution as an expression of divine wholeness. Faith is capable of holding the tension within the realization that one is both finite creature and eternal consciousness. Saniel Bonder, founder of a contemporary school of spiritual growth called the Waking Down movement, calls this tension the "core wound." It is seen by many to be the central problem of the spiritual life. Faith is its the ultimate solution.

Initial Wounding and Subsequent Development of Type Six

The inevitable failures of the holding environment during infancy threaten this sensitivity of the Six. Because the Six child's parents have themselves lost awareness of the ultimate ground of Faith, they cannot support such awareness in their child. They cannot trust that life itself will provide and instead feel that the child's future is entirely up to them. At some deep level they know they themselves cannot guarantee how life will be, and, of course, they do not trust the child to know, so they hover over the child with all of their doubts and fears. This makes them seem lacking and untrustworthy even when they offer good-enough parenting. And if their parenting truly fails to be good-enough, the Six child grows utterly terrified. It seems that the very people who are supposed to help one maintain contact with vital energy are themselves lacking the wisdom and/or the will to stay connected to it. Loss of the experience of being rooted in the life force leads to a sense that the external world is not only separate but that it is downright untrustworthy. The child grows ever more anxious, hypervigilant, and fearful. The Six's natural reconciling energy goes into overdrive as the child vacillates between fear of taking action and terror of remaining receptively open. As the vacillation vibrates faster and faster, a distortion of natural balance occurs, manifesting as both a narrowing and intensification of consciousness. The original awareness of unity shrinks until the ego can perceive only what seems threatening. Then it pumps up the threat and makes it bigger. When any source of energy is unbalanced, it becomes distorted. The distortion characteristic of reconciling energy is that it narrows its focus to only one partial segment of reality, which it then magnifies. Just as unbalanced absorbing energy becomes mired in inertia for Nines, and unbalanced expanding energy overflows into unrestrained excess for Threes, so the reconciling aspect of life energy characteristic of Sixes collapses into a narrower and narrower preoccupation with safety that actually ends up intensifying the perception of danger and insecurity.

The end product is a distorted version of Holy Faith, namely, a belief in caution and doubt as the only buffers against a predatory universe. The mind of a Six running on ego is a radar scanner searching for what will go wrong next. It feels to the unexamined Six that the scanning is a way of paying attention to everything, but actually it represents a collapse of consciousness. Only negative evidence is noticed, processed, and remembered. The mind of a Six may be constantly rotating like a searchlight, but its beam can be as narrow as the pupils of a frightened animal. And since all positive and hopeful evidence is excluded from the narrow sample, the conclusion that the universe is predatory seems constantly justified.

This conviction about the external world is in turn mirrored by a set of beliefs about the internal world. The Six, lacking contact with his own vital essence, comes to believe that he cannot rely on his own inner nature. It feels like there is nothing unshakeable inside. One's instincts are wrong, one's heart is false, and one's body is weak. As Sandra Maitri (2000) puts it, the Six feels that he is just a small hairless mammal with a large brain as his sole protection. This fear is the knothole experienced by the Six once contact with original energy is lost. And just as the Nine and the Three deal with their knotholes by going unconscious about them, the Six solves the problem of his knothole by excluding it from consciousness. The unexamined Six does not feel afraid: he thinks he is just trying to prevent all the things that could go wrong if he didn't pay attention to them!

The ego we Sixes constructed as we grew up had to find some way to regain our original loss. So in an act of sublime irony we adopted doubting as a substitute for Faith. Mental products replaced the direct knowing of the heart and belly. We became more and more preoccupied with security, prediction, and control. It was as though we were convinced that if we only knew what was coming next, we would always know when to duck. But even all that thinking could not put all of our fears to rest, for as good mental types, we knew that whatever the mind proposed, the mind could also repeal. No reasoning, no matter how careful or complete, was beyond counter argument. As a result we inevitably became preoccupied with authority. We wanted an authority so solid, steadfast, and certain as to be beyond our own questioning and doubting minds. But our early experiences of how we were failed by those who were supposed to guard and guide us had left us mistrustful of authority. So all we could do was to waver and stutter step—trying to believe yet always disbelieving. Ambivalence became the tattered remnant of the lost capacity to calmly hold the tension of finite and infinite within one gaze.

The endless anxiety generated by all of this ambivalence produced quite a bit of rage. But anger was too instinctual and too dangerous to be openly expressed. It might bring down the whole predatory universe upon our small, hairless animal self! Sometimes we just swallowed our anger and got tongue-tied. Other times we projected the anger outward critically attacking and judging others. Attacking others was actually just a misguided attempt to heal the situation. By attacking, we were trying to make others feel as misunderstood and hurt as we did, in the mistaken belief that once they felt sufficiently hurt, they would stop harassing us. In fact, we were the ones who needed to surrender to the hurt .

Point of Avoidance, Virtue, and Vice of Type Six

Our spiritual path as Sixes starts with the recognition of the automatic quality of our doubting, critical minds, and of how little certainty they produce. The next step has to do with turning inward, not into our heads, but into our hearts. What we will find there is fear. Each type is ruled by some fear. For example, Nines fear conflict, and Threes fear failure. What do we Sixes fear? Everything! Fear is the passion or vice that runs the entire structure of our type. We fear conflict, but we are also afraid when everything seems peaceful. We fear losing, but we also fear winning. We even are afraid of fear, which is the reason so many of us cannot recognize ourselves as Sixes. What is the root of all this fear? Oddly enough it has to do with the virtue of our type. Most books on the Enneagram call the virtue for type Six courage. I do not disagree with this, but I would like to specify it as the courage to trust. We are afraid to trust. Why? I have come to believe that we are terrified of trust because we so deeply *want* to trust. Our natural and spontaneous inclination is to trust, but our conditioned belief is that trusting has always led to catastrophe. So we eradicated the spontaneous inclination. In fact, we turned spontaneity into our point of avoidance. (I guess small, hairless mammals with oversize brains do not believe they can afford to be spontaneous.) If we are lucky, someday we will go below the fear and discover that we have always wanted nothing more than to trust and to be trusted in return. This is in truth one of our most beautiful qualities—our willingness to trust, especially to trust our own natural strength. Recognizing how we have fought against this quality with great determination may at first make us feel quite sad, but ultimately it will impart lasting relief. We can finally realize that the best part of our self has always been the most rejected part—and that we no longer have to keep playing this cruel trick on ourselves. Finally, we need to turn downward into our own body and to its instinctual wisdom and strength. Some Enneagram books say that Sixes need to shift toward Nine, the home of Holy Love, *yin* energy and a Body Type. More accurately, all types needs to undo the constriction and lack of balance that limit them to using one particular center of experience and one aspect of life energy. For Sixes, this means learning to trust that Being itself will take care of them. When Faith, the Holy Idea of Six is restored, Love and Hope appear, as well.

Pivot of Dao for Type Six

There is a deeply moving poem about trust written by Rainer Maria Rilke. Read it slowly, repeat its heavy lines frequently, and feel the ponderous weight of its grief:

> Perhaps I, like a single vein of ore, am inching
> through old sediment solidified in rock;
> so deeply in there is no end in sight,
> no open space. Everything seems too near,
> and everything near to me seems stone.
>
> As yet I am not skilled in heavy grief,
> so this colossal dark weighs down on me.
> But *Thou* art: brace thyself, breach my cave.
> Lay the full weight of thy hand on me,
> and I the buried depths of my soul on thee.

R.M. Rilke, *Das Stundenbuch*, translated by W. Schafer. The German text is as follows:

Vielleicht, dass ich durch schwere Berge gehe
in harten Adern, wie ein Erz allein;
und bin so tief, dass ich kein Ende sehe
und keine Ferne: alles wurde Nähe
und alle Nähe wurde Stein.

Ich bin ja noch kein Wissender im Wehe,--
so macht mich dieses grosse Dunkel klein;
bist Du *es aber: mach dich schwer, brich ein:*
dass deine ganze Hand an mir geschehe
und ich an dir mit meinem ganzen Schrein.

The turning point of the poem is the admission that one does not know how to proceed any further and the subsequent plea, "I am not yet skilled . . . but Thou art." The last word of the poem is a masterpiece of the ambiguity that opens up greater meaning. *Schrein* sounds like *Schrei*, which means cry of grief. I don't think Rilke chose *Schrein* simply to fulfill the requirements of the poem's rhyming scheme. The literal meaning of the word is cabinet. But it can also refer to an interior space, a shrine, or by extension a coffin. To cry out "Lay the full weight of thy hand on me, and I the buried depths of my soul on thee" is to make the greatest leap of faith—a giving of the most deeply vulnerable part of self to the fierce power of the universe. This is the *daoshu* for the Six. To the ego, the energy of fear and doubt and the energy of courage and strength seem opposite. Their unity appears only within the frictionlessness of no longer resisting them. What appears at that moment is quite surprising. I know something of this particular pivot, for I am a Type Six. There is a story I can tell you that may help explain how strength first unraveled into fear for me.

When I was small and I did something my mother had forbidden I would get a few whacks from the yard stick, which was kept in the milk closet by the back door. What I hated most about the yard stick was that I had to fetch it myself. The whipping was not that hard, for my mother was not brutal. But being made to participate in my own humiliation was demeaning beyond words. My older sister tells a story about the yard stick. She says that one day when she was six and I was between two and three, we both got into trouble together. My mother commanded me to fetch the yardstick. My sister recounts that I went to the milk closet, brought the stick to my mother—and broke it in front of her. She swears the look on our mother's face was one she had never seen before. It was a look of confusion. According to my sister, I received no punishment for this act of rebellion.

It is curious as well as a matter of great sadness to me that I have absolutely no memory of this event. I have heard the story, and I believe that it actually occurred, but it feels like a story told about someone else. In some sense it *is* a story about someone else. It is a story about a child who trusted his own strength in a way that I could no longer recognize as an adult. It was the power I could access before I became "me," whose story was that he was Billy the fearful child. Before he appeared, apparently I could be spontaneously courageous. But that kind of trust in my own strength could not long survive in our home. I loved my mother dearly, and I needed her to love me in return. She could not have tolerated the kind of energy I possessed at the age of two,[6] so I lay it down for her—for us, really. And later, when I had become the fearful child, my worst dread was really not (as it seemed) my mother's power to punish. What I feared most was my own strength, which I thought had the power to separate us. Like Rilke I thought, "Perhaps (nothing is certain for a Six!) the vein of ore I sought (security) could be found only by inching along through solidified rock (my mother's seemingly endless requirements). But the real rock was within, not around me. It lay so close to my face that there was actually nothing to separate it from me. What I lacked was not power as it turns out. It was being "skilled in heavy grief," the sadness of realizing that it was precisely my own strength that I had surrendered out of misguided love.

If this was my childhood path of rendering courage into fear, what would be my adult passageway for transforming fear back into courage? What I have found (I cannot say with any certainty that it will be

6 I now watch my youngest grandson. His energy is if anything stronger than the one I possessed. Butting heads with him I have come to a new and more compassionate understanding for my mother!

exactly the same for all Sixes) is that when I notice fear—usually it has to do with confronting someone who is important to me—if I simply stay with the experience, remaining still and welcoming, I begin to notice that just inside or perhaps below the fear is an expansive energy that feels quite powerful, even fierce. That's my power. That is what I most deeply fear. If I remain quite still I can literally feel the energy running in both directions at once—one side toward fear, the other toward power. At some point they become almost indistinguishable and I begin to feel sad. If I simply let go the tension between them disappears, the sadness melts, and courage to move ahead with faith appears in its place. I no longer have to manage the tension and can let the energy run as it wants to. Thus I find that I have greater access not only to the *yin* receptivity of my central triangle partner Nine but to the *yang* energy of Three, as well. In this way the entire triangle seems to come together—as I suspect it does for any other type once in the *daoshu*. Holy Faith, once reawakened, leads also to renewed Hope and Love.

Chapter 5:

Types Five, Eight, and Two

Figure 9:
Types Five, Eight, and Two

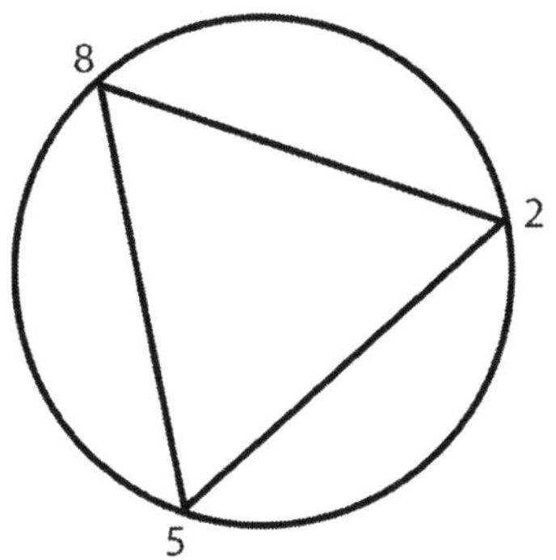

The traditional manner of presenting the remaining six types is to follow the order of the Enneagram's irregular hexagon: One, Four, Two, Eight, Five, and Seven. For reasons that will become clearer as we go, I am not going to do that. Instead, I will next describe the types forming the equilateral triangle of Five, Two, and Eight, and in the following chapter present the last triangle comprised of types Four, Seven, and One. Although this is not the currently familiar manner of rendering the Enneagram, once one is aware of the *yin*, *yang*, and reconciling energetic aspects of the nine types, it quickly becomes apparent that the equilateral triangles formed by types Five, Eight, and Two and by types Four, Seven, and One are structurally identical to the inner triangle formed by types Nine, Six, and Three. Each triangle contains one member in each center of experience: one that is unbalanced *yin*, one that is unbalanced *yang*, and one that is unbalanced reconciling. As these three triangles come more closely into focus, some very interesting relationships will appear.

TYPE FIVE

Holy Idea: Omniscience and Transparency

The life energy of Enneatype Five, like that of Nine, is unbalanced toward *yin*. At first this might seem strange to those of you who are not Fives. From the outside, Fives can seem so withdrawn and socially isolated that is it hard to see how they can be *yin*. But this is only because many people limit their understanding of *yin* energy to receptivity in the arena of social relationships. The Five is extremely receptive and *yin*, but in the mental arena rather than the social. If you doubt this, just watch a Five open a book. To a Five, a book is a sacred object to be absorbed whole in its entirety.

The Enneagram tradition describes the Holy Idea of Type Five with two names: Holy Omniscience and Holy Transparency. Holy Omniscience refers to the spiritual intuition that everything is an expression of one original awareness. Holy Transparency refers to the perception that every individual being is totally and completely illuminated by that same awareness. Enneatype Five, like its neighbor Six, is one of the mental types. But unlike Six, whose energy is reconciling, the energy of the Five is *yin*. Its mental way of processing experience is to merge with whatever is known and that gives the knowledge of Type Five an interior perspective. A Five knows, not so much by analyzing and dissecting, but by joining with the known object, perceiving it as though the Five were on the inside looking out. Omniscience in this context therefore does not mean "knowing everything about everything." It means "knowing whatever is known totally, from the inside." This is very similar to the classical Chinese notion of *ming* (to illuminate). To illuminate is not the same as to know. Knowing (*zhi*) is accomplished by the *xin* or the heart-mind and results in knowledge derived from principles and concepts. To *ming* is to know something concretely, in its individuality. The word *ming* can mean "bright" as in a bright object, "insightful" as in insightful observer, and most fundamentally *both at once,* as in a well-illumined situation. *Ming* is what happens whenever one accesses the Pivot of Dao. As we shall see later on, the great Daoist sage *Zhuangzi* uses *ming* somewhat humorously to mean "following the obvious." (Or at least his translator did.)

From this vantage point, Omniscience is seen to be a whole-being knowing that makes Fives particularly aware of the porous transparency of all the walls that seem to separate individual beings. If the field of *Qi* is like an ocean, Fives know it from a vantage point inside one of its droplets. Their special sensitivity is to intuitively realize that each drop is indistinguishable from the ocean itself.

Initial Wounding and Subsequent Development for Type Five

The failures of the holding environment in infancy threaten these sensitivities. Many Fives seem to experience a double failure of mothering. The first occurs with embodiment itself. They seem to feel that the very first entity to hold them—gravity—was an awkward mother and that they have never been quite comfortable in her arms. Some of them additionally feel that their own parents were either invasive or not present. Either way, their experience was that they were never really "held." Accordingly, many Fives grow up feeling emotionally unconnected to those around them. The resulting knothole is a sense of pervasive emptiness surrounded by walls that seem too fragile either to contain the emptiness or to protect it from being exploited.

If this was your early experience, your initial defensive reaction was to withdraw. You hid in an attempt to protect yourself. You became preoccupied with boundaries. You became almost the reverse image of your fellow *yin* type, Nine, for whom any boundary seems like an impenetrable wall. For you as a Five, it seemed that no boundary would ever be impermeable enough to keep you safe. The preoccupation with boundaries was the first distortion of Holy Transparency. In order to keep the boundaries secure, you learned to withdraw and to make do with less because that made you feel less dependent upon others. The parsimony of your existence gave you a sense of safety, but it ultimately heightened your feelings of emptiness and separateness, as well.

Under your disconnectedness from life lay a vague sense of guilt for not having known something. It is as though you believed that had you only known better, you would have been able to woo your parents better so that they would know you with the same interiority with which you wanted to know them. The guilt over not knowing them led you down a lifelong quest to gather information and to attain knowledge. In this way you attempted to recreate the lost essential quality of Holy Omniscience. Your emphasis, however, was primarily placed on attaining and owning rather than on adapting and utilizing knowledge. Moving out into the world with what you knew seemed too dangerous, for it could expose your inner life to others. Once you gathered the information for yourself, you felt little need to do much else with it. This represented a further distortion of receptive energy, from interior whole-being knowing to a kind of intellectual withdrawal from real life.

The disconnection from life also brought a disconnection from others' energy. Rather than exchanging energy with other people you withdrew because you thought any exchange would drain your own energy. Thus you experienced periods of feeling barely alive. This inner sense of running on dry tanks supported your emotional "vice" as a Five, which is called avarice or stinginess. Stinginess results from the choking off of your original receptive energy. It represents the Five's version of the inertia seen in all *yin* types when their energy becomes unbalanced. If you are a Five, when you are asked to reveal something about yourself or to engage emotionally with someone, your first instinct is probably to flee or to shut down. It feels as though granting the request will require too much time and energy and will expose you to being drained by the petitioner's demands. You have this feeling in part because you are so deeply aware of how any one piece of your being is connected to all the others. It seems that sharing any one part of yourself will inevitably require you to share and/or give away everything else. Otherwise, you will have given the other person only a partial glimpse of who you are, and they may not understand it. They might come to false conclusions about you—and you might not ever know what those are. Thus you end up paralyzed by the belief that you have only two choices—either you conceal yourself and give nothing away, or you tell all and offer everything. This is just another version of the law of inertia. It operates similarly to that of Nines who can't get started once they are at rest and have a hard time stopping once they are in action.

The inertia of stinginess inevitably left you with the feeling that you were living in a parched desert with barely enough supplies to keep life going. So your natural instinct was to collect, hoard, and accumulate. The paradox was that though you consciously thought yourself detached, you were, in fact, taking pride in your ability to make do with so little. You were probably quite unaware that your primary attachment was actually to feeling detached. This attachment had become the ultimate distortion of your soul's original *yin* receptivity.

Once again I turn to Rabindranath Tagore for a description of your dilemma. He paints for us a picture of one who knows but cannot make contact:

> I know thee as my God and stand apart—
> I do not know thee as my own and come closer.
> I know thee as my father and bow before thy feet—
> I do not grasp thy hand as my friend's.
>
> I stand not where thou comest down
> and ownest thyself as mine,
> there to clasp thee to my heart
> and take thee as my comrade.
> Thou are the Brother amongst my brothers,
> but I heed them not,
> I divide not my earnings with them,
> thus sharing my all with thee.
> In pleasure and in pain I stand not by the side of men,
> and thus stand by thee.
> I shrink to give up my life,
> and thus do not plunge into the great waters of life.

Rabindranath. Tagore, *Gitanjali*, No. 77.

Point of Avoidance, Virtue, and Vice of Type for Type Five

The virtue for type Five is traditionally called Nonattachment. My wife Alice, a Five, suggests that Nonattachment falls slightly short of describing the actual virtue for her type. She proposes that Generosity may be better suited to name the original energy that is squeezed until it turns into Avarice. I tend to agree. Nonattachment seems such a neutral term. Technically, that is not quite true, of course. Nonattachment differs from detachment in that it neither rejects nor selects. It simply remains open to everything. Nonetheless, nonattachment may be a better description of the Five's Pivot of Dao than of its virtue. Nonattachment is the place of no resistance that allows for spontaneous movement of true generosity, which is the freedom to either protect oneself from harmful intrusion or offer oneself in a gesture of service, according to the flow of the situation rather than according to the habits of the ego.

Entry into that pivot, as always, requires repeated surrendering to one's point of avoidance. The point of avoidance for a Five is called Emptiness. At first, this may seem mystifying. When Fives begin to take up the Enneagram's suggested path of development, it often seems that the experience to be avoided is not so much emptiness, but being "too full"—too full of feelings, too full of things to do, too full of noise and distraction. With a little more practice, however, it gets clearer that the fear of "too full" is rooted in the belief that intense feelings, busy schedules, and high levels of activity or excitement will drain the Five's meager resources until the Five is totally depleted.

Pivot of Dao for Type Five

What does emptiness mean in this context? First of all, it means the emptiness of *not knowing*. Not knowing is more than just not having the answer. Searching for a shop I have never visited before, I may come to an unfamiliar intersection. I don't know whether to turn right or left. This is not true not knowing, for at least I know one alternative will be correct. The not knowing of emptiness is totally without content. It is a pregnant silence that like uncarved wood can become . . . *anything*! Secondly, the emptiness of Five's point of avoidance has an energetic quality. The Five's deepest fear is that others will deplete her of the little energy she has, leaving her without vital substance. Therefore, in order to enter into the Pivot of Dao, the Five must voluntarily experience the energetic emptiness of being willing to surrender everything. Chapter

11 of the *Daodejing* describes emptiness as the essential quality of the Pivot of Dao:

> The thirty spokes converge at one hub,
> But the utility of the cart is a function of the nothingness (*wu*) inside the hub.
> We throw clay to shape a pot,
> But the utility of the clay pot is a function of the nothingness inside it.
> We bore out doors and windows to make a dwelling,
> But the utility of the dwelling is a function of the nothingness inside it.

Dao is the ultimate emptiness. It is said to be identity without shape and meaning without form. What does that mean? The phrase identity without shape means that as underlying Field, *Dao* is everywhere yet nowhere. *Dao* is within everything yet is no thing. In this sense *Dao* can be said to be empty, yet it is this emptiness that gives meaning or be-ing to each *de*, or individual focus. Each *de* in turn is shape without identity (form without meaning). That is, no *de* of itself has real meaning except insofar as it participates in *Dao*. The unique genius of Daoism is that it did not turn *Dao* into the creator or cause of *de*. Instead it realized that *Dao* cannot exist without *de* any more than *de* can exist without *Dao*. They are two fundamentally and eternally co-implicated aspects of all that is or ever could be. This is entirely consistent with the fundamental Daoist paradigm that apparent opposites are always mutually co-implicated. If we apply this to the situation of the Five, we find that emptiness and fullness are two mutually implied aspects of one underlying reality. That realization places one at the very heart of the Five's Pivot of Dao.

The spiritual task of the Five is to take this last paragraph and translate it from concepts into lived experience. The drop into emptiness is not, as the Five's ego fears, a fall into self-annihilation. The ego, particularly our western version of it, divides everything into Being and Non-Being. It believes that emptiness is Non-Being or nothingness and is terrified of it. But when we experience rather than think about emptiness, we find that it is not nothingness; it is presence. However, it is presence without form. Experiencing emptiness therefore does not mean feeling nothing; it is experiencing a type of presence but one that has no content. And formless presence, although empty of content, requires a response from the one who experiences it. The response is not one of knowing—that simply turns the formless into some sort of content. The proper response to formless presence is welcome, gratitude, and greeting. There is a marvelous poem by the contemporary British (now living in Canada) poet-philosopher David Whyte which deeply explores this. The poem's title is "It is Not Enough."

> It is not enough to know.
> It is not enough to follow
> the inward road conversing in secret.
>
> It is not enough to see straight ahead,
> to gaze at the unborn
> thinking the silence belongs to you.
>
> It is not enough to hear
> even the tiniest edge of rain.
>
> You must go to the place
> where everything waits,
> there, when you finally rest,
> even one word will do,
> one word or the palm of your hand
> turning outward
> in the gesture of gift.
>
> And now we are truly afraid
> to find the great silence
> asking so little.
>
> One word, one word only.

David Whyte, *Where Many Rivers Meet,* 1990. Reprinted by permission of the author.

The poem is telling us that you can study for years, you can become a supremely good meditator, you can quiet the ordinary mind, and still you may not have reached true inner freedom. You must go to the place where *everything* waits. In that place, when you finally stop resisting, the smallest gesture will suffice. The gesture must come from the heart, not the head. It is directed to someone or something other than oneself. Yet in that small movement of self-emptying, the

Five discovers that true fullness of illumination lives hidden within the immense longing of his own heart. Each time the Five enters this pivot it becomes that much easier to share his interior awareness of the Brother's presence to all brothers. And this is how the Five eventually reclaims Holy Omniscience and Transparency.

TYPE EIGHT

Holy Idea: Truth

The Holy Idea of type Eight is called Holy Truth. Truth in this context has nothing to do with propositional accuracy. It is not about the truth of any concept or idea. Type Eight shares the creative and expansive energy of type Three since type Eight also possess an energy that is unbalanced toward *yang*. However, the Eight is a body type and experiences the energy viscerally rather than emotionally. The Eight infant's experience of Holy Truth is one of gut level openness to the life energy's quality of *authentic presence.* Truth is the intuited certainty that the entire field of *Qi* is one buzzing, sizzling actuality that cannot ever be divided or diminished. Sandra Maitri points out that Holy Truth is the awareness that nothing that happens in one part of the field can in any fundamental way be opposed to anything happening in any other part. Truth is the instinctive experience of the life force as a wholeness that is simultaneously indivisible and multidimensional and the immediate awareness that this energy cannot ever move *against* itself. In this sense, Holy Truth is almost a mirror image of type Five's Holy Omniscience and Transparency. Recall that the Five infant is most sensitive to how each part the *Qi* field interpenetrates every other. This is also true of the Eight infant. But whereas the focus of the Five is more from the inside looking out, the focus of the Eight is from the outside looking in. The Five knows the ocean wholly from within one drop of water; the Eight senses the entire ocean at once.

Initial Wounding and Subsequent Development of Type Eight

The Eight infant, sensitive as he is to the original energy's dynamic unity, experiences embodiment into a universe physically dispersed into time and space as a tremendous threat. Many Eights I have known carry a conscious memory of a time when it seemed they were about to be annihilated out of being. I believe many other Eights carry this as an unconscious trauma. It is as though the Eight infant came to feel that some part of Being was opposed to his own being and lost sight of his indivisible energetic unity to it as a result. As Holy Truth was lost, the Eight felt progressively more cut off from the wholeness of the life force, lost in one tiny physical body floating in a sea of dualities. The result was the arising of a strong sense of separateness: self vs. other, right vs. wrong, light vs. dark, male vs. female, human vs. divine. It seemed to the young Eight that a terrible thing had happened. He didn't know what this terrible thing was; he simply sensed that something was profoundly wrong. To make matters worse, the Eight felt that he had allowed this terrible thing to happen, was personally responsible for the loss, and thus personally obliged to redress it.

If you are an Eight, it was around such a knothole that your ego crystallized. Given your tendency to process experience kinesthetically, you transformed the intuition that something bad had happened into an almost visceral sense of being bad yourself. Given that you possessed a type of energy that naturally moves outward, you then projected that sense of badness onto the world. You transformed guilt into blame—after all, better to blame someone else than yourself. Your natural way of relating to the world was to engage directly, and blaming others simply transformed that tendency into a propensity to engage through attack. As you turned more and more outward, you became more and more unconscious, or to use Gurdjiev's term, you fell more deeply asleep. In order to restore some sense of your lost inner source of energy you created a counterfeit version of it—a passion for excess and over-the-top living, called Lust, which is the vice of type Eight. Lust represented the ultimate distortion of your original *yang* energy. Underneath, you avoided at all costs any feeling of being a vulnerable, hurt child.

The fundamental illusion of type Eight is that life is war. Since the ego believes that Being is "against" its continued survival, the ego thinks it can survive only by being "against" what seems threatening, unjust, or wrong. It is like the collective madness we encounter in nations or cultures that have been fighting one another for centuries. Each attack is responded to with a counter-attack in the illusory belief that only continued aggression will protect security and produce peace. It is the mindset of the warrior who returns from the front unable to live an ordinary life. His senses have been sharpened to watch for every sign of danger and his instincts honed to respond quickly and without thinking. The quietness of ordinary life seems almost unbearable, and he is likely to stir up trouble simply to make the outside world correspond better to his inner vision of it.

In spiritual work, Eights are often tempted to believe that they are in a veritable battle for their soul. The battle is at root a war to overcome duality. They feel compelled to conquer the feeling that good and evil are divided. This sense that good and evil have been divided can show up in one of two ways. In the first way, Eights can believe the division lies within their own soul, and they battle with it there. In the second way, they feel that the war is between them and those who are less enlightened, and they carry the battle outward. Either way, what stands between them and the perception of Holy Truth is the *battle.* What is this battle really about? And is it still necessary?

Point of Avoidance, Virtue and Vice of Type for Type Eight

Essentially, it is the battle of *yang* against *yin*, of power versus innocence. The inner world of the Eight is stretched out on this dimension more tightly than on any other. The egoic life of an Eight is all about power. The short version of its worldview is that power must at all costs suppress frailty or some unbearable evil will occur. The passion here is called Lust, or Excess. It is a surge of unbalanced *yang* energy that believes it is confronted by evil and is trying to do whatever it can to crush it. At a deeper level, the passion is trying also to crush any lingering *yin* childhood tendency to be receptive. Yet that same energy of the passion, when released, can transform into the virtue of type Eight, called Innocence. Innocence (from the Latin *in-nocens* or not harming) meets the apparition of evil without any wish to destroy. It may instinctively parry and deflect the evil thrust, but it does not feel any need to kill it. Standing between the Eight's passion and virtue is its point of avoidance, Vulnerability. (The word comes from the Latin *vulnus* meaning wound). Feeling wounded, even for a moment, brings up the whole weight of the Eight's childhood fear of being annihilated.

And right behind that fear is a deep sense of personal blame for having let oneself be weak. The Eight's ego still believes that only sheer force can prevent him from getting hurt. It does not understand that all energy, even that which seems evil, is an expression of one creative surge. And it surely cannot see that one of the greatest dangers to the Eight's adult well being may be the loaded gun inside his own belly.

Pivot of Dao for Type Eight

Entrance into the Pivot of Dao for type Eight begins with the realization that there is an element of weakness within all strength and a core of strength within all weakness. Strength is what is beginning to weaken; weakness is what is beginning to grow strong. If an Eight resides willingly within his point of avoidance for any length of time, he will begin to understand this. At first it is extremely difficult to allow, even for a moment, any small sense of vulnerability. Feeling vulnerable immediately throws the ego toward the *yin* side of the still point, and the *yang* reaction is immediate. The trick is to find the *daoshu*, the point of still attention to the ego's madness that begins to create a space around the madness. In this space the Eight will discover his childhood innocence. He can stop making war on weakness and begin to feel compassion toward himself for having once been small. He will begin to realize that even though he was once temporarily draped in a small child's body, his essential being was never weak or insignificant. The formless presence which is "I"—Being- Loving-Aware—is boundless and capable of holding the entire cosmos. To experience for oneself the spaciousness that can hold such wholeness is to recover Holy Truth.

Laozi knew something of this. Earlier I quoted chapter 55 of the *Daodejing*, which begins with this description of the Sage:

> One who is vital in character (*de*)
> Can be compared with a newborn baby.
>
> Wasps and scorpions will not sting a baby,
> Snakes and vipers will not bite him,
> And birds of prey and ferocious beasts will not snatch him up.
> Though his bones are soft and his sinews supple
> His grip is firm.

As yet oblivious to the copulation of male and female
His member still stands erect:
Such is the height of potency. (*de*)

If you recall, *de* is the present individual focus of the field, or *Dao*. Each *de* is unique and unrepeatable. The purpose of its existence is to *ziran*, or to "self-so." This means that the destiny of each *de* is to become more and more fully what it is. The passage quoted asserts that the sage is like an infant in that he possesses a power that is neither masculine nor feminine. The text does not however specifically describe how this power becomes even more fully vital or "self-so" in the adult sage. Fortunately, Thomas Merton, the Catholic Christian mystic, further elaborated *Laozi's* insight for us. He wrote that each soul is a unique word spoken by God and that the spiritual task of each person is to learn the meaning of this word and speak it to the world. Like *Laozi*, Merton was aware that the soul was born fully complete, but he added the important insight that the infant must develop an adult personality before it can announce that fullness to the rest of humanity. The grown Eight, choosing to remain within the still point that is neither weak nor strong is contemplating the full significance of his own *de*. As the Eight further undergoes the alchemy of spiritual growth, he will come to see that the capacity to be consciously vulnerable leads, not to impotence and defeat, but to a power so refined by the fierce fire of Truth that it never needs to harm. This is freedom to be truly innocent.

I want to make this complicated but important point in a more emotionally compelling way, so I turn again to David Whyte who affirms in beautifully strong modern declaratives the Pivot of Dao for reclaiming Holy Truth in a poem called "Self Portrait."

It doesn't interest me if there is one God
or many gods.
I want to know if you belong or feel
abandoned.
If you know despair or can see it in others.
I want to know
if you are prepared to live in the world
with its harsh need
to change you. If you can look back
with firm eyes

saying this is where I stand. I want to know
if you know
how to melt into that fierce heat of living
falling toward
the center of your longing. I want to know
if you are willing
to live, day by day with the consequence of love
and the bitter
unwanted passion of your sure defeat.

I have been told, in *that* fierce embrace, even
the gods speak of God.

David Whyte, *Fire in the Earth*, 1992. Reprinted by permission of the author.

The poet is telling us that the real defeat is to divide rather than to belong. Dividing means fighting against the world and trying to keep it at bay rather than living in the world and being changed by it. Belonging means allowing oneself to feel despair. The real victory is to stand firm while melting toward the still center of one's longing. For an Eight, such melting is the realization that everything falls inexorably toward a common unity. Its movement may be fierce indeed, but it is the consequence of love. There is no need for war. One can be both true and harmless. From this frictionless perspective, the holy warrior is like an infant. He is soft and supple, yet beyond all harm. He does not fight a war of separation; he does not divide reality into opposites. He does not engage in the battle of *yin* and *yang*. And as a result they, like twin gods, begin to speak of one Truth.

TYPE TWO

Holy Idea: Will and Freedom

Type Two is the second triangle's exemplar of unbalanced reconciling energy. The Holy Idea of Enneatype Two has two names: Holy Will and Holy Freedom. Holy Will is the awareness that the life force is intentional and purposeful in the way that it unfolds, particularly with regard to oneself. It is the intuition that the divine process is concerned with my personal destiny. It is a perception particularly focused upon the fundamental interrelatedness of the divine wholeness and the particularity that is *me*. Hence the energy of type Two is fundamentally reconciling, just like type Six. However, now that concern with balance is being expressed by an emotional or heart type.

Holy Will therefore implies that the infant Two naturally intuits the life energy's deep concern for every creature's growth and development. However this intuition of how divine creativity intersects with human destiny is not understood by the perennial philosophy as predestination. Predestination is a belief that everything happens according to some prefixed plan in the mind of an anthropomorphically conceptualized God. Although such a god is usually stated to be eternal, in actual practice it is imagined as existing in time—with the exception that its time is always ahead of our own. From the viewpoint of Holy Will, there is no preordained plan because time itself is understood to be an illusion. Each moment unfolds meaningfully out of the previous but cannot be foreseen prior to actually coming into being. According to this view, unfoldment occurs as pure expression of the one timeless *Dao*. Only to the human mind does it seem to be stretched out in time.

Holy Freedom is the subjective effect of perceiving Holy Will. If a person is fully aware of the direction and momentum of the life force, she will experience her life as an unfolding of her own specific destiny. She knows she is being moved (more precisely that she is one with the movement) to become more "self-so," or more fully the *de* she individually is and that this is her fundamental way of serving the needs of the whole. Her realization that she is this meant to be *de* within the eternal process of *Dao* is what makes her *free*.[7]

7 In Old English "free" originally meant "beloved." In ancient times, the beloved of the king was "*freij,*" meaning that person was exempt from taxation. In modern German, a baroness is called a *Freifrau* (literally a "beloved woman"). The verb *freien* means "to woo," and the fifth day of the week, named for the goddess of love, is *Freitag* from which we derive our English word "Friday."

Initial Wounding and Subsequent Development for Type Two

This awareness cannot be maintained, however, given that the Two's caregivers have themselves lost awareness of their connection to essence, the fullness of energy. Its loss leaves the young Two feeling adrift without any sense of inner direction. She feels insignificant and invisible. It seems that the life force has forgotten *her*. This sense of being unimportant and unlovable becomes the knot around which her personality crystallizes. Recall however that the ego constructed to untie this knot is an ego that processes experience by seeking emotional connection to the world. As a heart type, the Two is fundamentally oriented to other humans. The Two's sense of self is acutely attuned to others and to their reactions. But since its energy is unbalanced toward reconciling, the ego tries to control the balance of *yin* and *yang* rather than allowing it to happen naturally. This leaves the young Two uncomfortably pinned between the needs of self and the needs of others, between egoism and altruism. She cannot actively compete for love like a Three—that would feel too *yang*. But she cannot sit back and wait for love come to her like a Nine might do, for that would feel too *yin*. She must instead find a way to get others to love her without appearing to intentionally do so. Her way out of the dilemma is to find people whose needs only she can supply and in that way make herself indispensable. In this way altruism can serve the needs of egoism. As a result, just as the reconciling energy of the Six collapsed into a narrow preoccupation with security, the Two's energy collapses into an intense effort to care for others while unconsciously calling attention to self.

Since the Two feels so adrift inside, the energy for all this activity has to be found in others. It leaves her compulsively preoccupied with what others need and almost incapable of noticing her own deeper needs. This compulsion may sometimes appear as a search for romantic intimacy expressed either through perpetually seeking new lovers or perhaps in the midst of a stable married life through preoccupation with romance novels, soap operas, or sentimental displays. Sometimes it shows up as a predilection for babies and children and a penchant for offering them all the pleasures of childhood, which the Two can then vicariously enjoy. Sometimes it takes the form of co-dependency and an inability to set proper limits upon the behavior and demands of others. No matter how it is expressed, the distinctive way Twos bind themselves to each Special Someone is by taking care of them and tending to their needs. It is their way of trying to rediscover their own inner worth by "importing" it from others.

This may sound very much like what we described earlier about the Nine who forgets self and gets lost in others. But the Two's energy feels quite different. Both Enneatypes experience others as more important than self. Their attention goes outward. But the Nine's energy is resting and receptive whereas the Two's energy is preoccupied and concerned. For example, a Nine at a cocktail party may just stand there until someone comes up to talk to him. Then he might temporarily get lost in that person's story and agenda. A Two at the same party will unconsciously scan the room for that one person who seems needy or depressed (or quite conversely, who seems vital and important, and in need of a first-rate promoter or agent) and make a bee-line for that person. The behavior of a Two running on ego power always feels far more intensely focused than that of a Nine.

Point of Avoidance, Virtue, and Vice of Type of Type Two

If you are a Two, your habit of finding people to care for made you feel temporarily important because so many people seemed to need you. You instinctively knew what people liked, and it felt good to you to give it to them. It made you popular. Sometimes, however, it felt rather burdensome. Frantically trying to feed other people in order to make them fill your own inner flatness only creates exhaustion in the long run. At first it was probably hard for you to recognize this since you experienced such intense pleasure in the course of caring for others. The pleasure consisted in a secret pride, a feeling that only you knew what they needed and could give it to them. (If you recall, Pride is the passion of the Two fixation.) Of course, you had to keep any direct expression of pride tightly repressed for self-centeredness was not supposed to be a part of the image you projected out to the world as a giving Two. But the pleasure of giving to others in a way that promised some reward of gratitude for yourself remained as the counterfeit imitation of your essential spiritual connection to Holy Will and Freedom.

The virtue or unconstricted energy for Type Two is called Humility. Ichazo defines it as the "acceptance of the limits of the body, its capacities." Helen Palmer defines it as the "ability to look into a mirror and feel grateful for exactly what one sees." Humility exposes one's self-image of helpfulness as a manipulative illusion. At first, however, it may be difficult for Twos to distinguish humility from humiliation. The confusion of humility with humiliation makes it very hard for Twos to simply stay still when they feel needy. The experience of personal need is in fact type Two's point of avoidance. Personal need makes Twos think they have nothing to give, and this brings up feelings of deep shame: "If I have nothing to give, I am worthless." This collapse into worthlessness is the Two's version of the collapse of energy which we have seen to be characteristic of all the reconciling energy types when their energy becomes egoic. Energy collapses into a narrow preoccupation with a small sector of experience and then magnifies it all out of proportion. For type Two, the narrow preoccupation focuses on what someone else needs and seems unable to do for himself. That need is then magnified until it becomes all the Two can see. Underneath lies an unrecognized magnification of the Two's importance to the other person.

And what is the basic spiritual longing under all of this? As for all the heart types, it is the wish to be connected. The Two feels she has lost her original connection to Source. The sense of personal unworthiness left over from this loss seems too deep to bear. The longing to be filled by something or someone else seems so overwhelmingly *yin* that the Two recoils from it. But she also shrinks from any direct attempt to claim her personal worth and ask for what she wants because that seems too *yang*. And like a ball falling down a narrowing well ricocheting from one wall to the other faster and faster, the tense vibration of personal unworthiness vs. wish for connection collapses into the narrowly focused energy of the Two's preoccupation with giving and getting.

Pivot of Dao for Type Two

The pivot of Dao for any of the reconciling types is the still point midway through each oscillation. This becomes possible only if you cease to resist the tension itself. The only reason the ball ricochets off the walls of the well is that it fails to fall straight down. Giving yourself fully to the plunge, allowing gravity to do the work, is how you enter into the pivot point. You stop trying to "act lovable" and simply allow love to act. This means giving up the illusion that you can own or produce love and sinking into the realization that love owns and produces you.

The truth of the matter is that one is truly free (beloved) only when one stops trying to create one's lovableness so as to "own" it. The process of healing for the Two begins with the realization that failing to allow those around her to give to her as they would like is really a cruel theft, taking from them the very means of showing her how much they love her. As this insight matures, she can become more comfortable allowing them to give to her because she now understands that this is perhaps the greatest gift she herself has to bestow. One day that realization will ripen into a lived awareness that the depth of our spiritual neediness actually proclaims and validates the profundity of our original connection to Source. Suppose you come to a situation like one described earlier in Chapter 3. You are a parent who has done so much for your child, and your child fails to even call you on your birthday. How do you use such a crisis to access your pivot of Dao? Neither complain to your partner, nor think of some way to indirectly remind your child that it is your birthday, nor pick up the phone to lay a guilt trip. Just remain still and feel the hurt. If you smile inwardly at the feeling, you will gradually create a small space around it. The reason the space appears is that you are no longer identified as the aggrieved parent; you have become the observer of the one feeling aggrieved. In that space you may begin to observe the humiliation transform into something else—the realization that your hunger to be loved and appreciated originates most deeply in your longing to be totally and fully aware of your connection to the Source of love that made you. The paradox revealed in the Two's Pivot of Dao is that it is precisely the self's emptiness that makes it capable of containing the divine Other. Listen once more to Tagore:

Thus it is that thy joy in me is so full.
Thus it is that thou hast come down to me.
O thou lord of all heavens,
where would be thy love if I were not?

Thou hast taken me as thy partner of all this wealth.
In my heart is the endless play of thy delight.
In my life thy will is ever taking shape.

And for this, thou who art the King of kings
hast decked thyself in beauty to captivate my heart.
And for this thy love
loses itself in the love of thy lover,
and there art thou seen
in the perfect union of two.

Rabindranath Tagore, *Gitanjali*, No. 56

Chapter 6:

Types Four, Seven, and One

Figure 10:
Types Four, Seven, and One

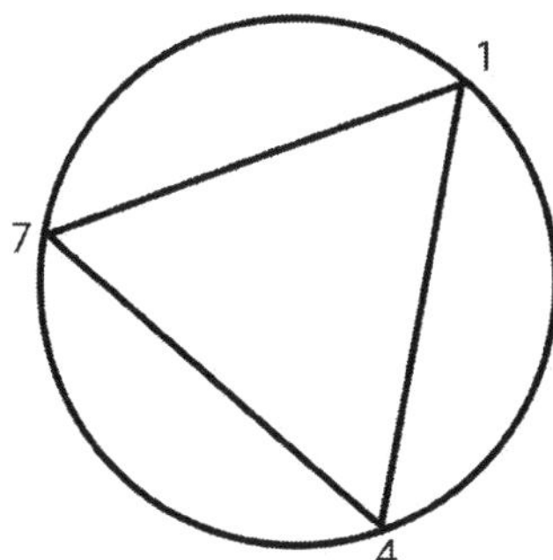

The last three Enneatypes form yet a third equilateral triangle. Like the first two triangles, one member is predominantly unbalanced toward *yin*, a second is predominantly unbalanced toward *yang*, while the last is predominantly unbalanced toward reconciling *yin* and *yang*. However in this final triangle, the type characterized by excess *yin* energy is found among the heart types (type Four), the type that runs on excess *yang* energy within the head types (type Seven), and the type trying to force a balance between the two is found within the body types (type One). Thus when we complete this last triangle we will have encountered each energy type once within each center of experience.

TYPE FOUR

Holy Idea: Origin

The Holy Idea of type Four is called Origin. It may seem an odd word at first. Origin refers to the awareness that all physical and psychological forms spring from one formless Source. The particular shading of this intuition results from the Four's unique blending of receptive *yin* energy with a heart type's emotional manner of experiencing reality. The intuition of Holy Origin is a felt awareness of one's connection to the field of *Qi*. It is the intuition that one's deepest authenticity and worth originate in one's connection to the divine mystery itself. This implies far more than the usual understanding of "We are all God's creatures." The deepest perception of Holy Origin is a whole-being awareness that the Divine Unknown, the "All-That-Is-or-Could-Be" is also being *you*. You are It. In this sense, the original awareness of the Four is extremely close to the conscious experience of waking up or being enlightened. The great fourteenth-century Persian poet Hafiz gives a somewhat whimsical description of this awareness in the following poem:

YOU'RE IT

God
Disguised
As a myriad things and
Playing a game
Of tag
Has kissed you and said,
"You're it –
I mean, you're Really IT!"

Now
It does not matter
What you believe or feel
For something wonderful,
Major-league Wonderful
Is someday going
To
Happen.

From the Penguin publication *The Gift, Poems by Hafiz the Great Sufi Master,* copyright 1999 Daniel Ladinsky and used with his permission.

Initial Wounding and Subsequent Development of Type Four

If you are a Four, you were born with this background awareness but gradually lost it in part through the experience of being cared for by parents who could not perceive the heart dimension of your true essence since they had lost the ability to recognize their own. You then experienced the loss as though it were abandonment, a loss of connection with the life force itself. What was left was a knothole that felt like a sense of deep deficiency. The ego that crystallized around this knothole was convinced that something terribly important was missing and withdrew into an endless preoccupation with retrieving what had been lost. As you grew up, you found yourself more and more enveloped by feelings of melancholy and longing for that unnamable person, thing, or quality that would make you whole.

You may be wondering how this is different from what you just read about the development of a Two. Both are heart types reacting to an experience of not being seen deeply at the level of the soul, which is the shock of embodiment common to emotional types. The Two ended up feeling like she had been forgotten. Now we are saying that Fours end up feeling that they have been abandoned. What is the distinction? The answer has to do with the differences between the narrowing collapse of consciousness that occurs within the reconciling energy of the Two and the collapse into inertia that happens to the receptive energy of the Four. If you are a Four, when you felt abandoned by the life force, you compensated for the personal aspect of what seemed lost, for example, the parent whom you experienced as abandoning, by taking the one you lost back into the self (psychologists would say that you introjected the lost object). That is, you identified emotionally with the one you felt you had lost and absorbed the memory of that person back into yourself once more. This early tendency toward introjection was perhaps the natural expression of your native predisposition to absorbing *yin* energy.

However, once the "abandoning" object took up residence within you, the unconscious anger you felt toward it inevitably began to feel like it was directed against yourself. You felt that you were not enough, that you were lacking something terribly important. In other words, you felt shame about yourself. You simultaneously imagined that others possessed whatever you were missing, and you experienced a sense of growing envy toward them. As a result, your wide-open *yin* heart energy began to constrict. You wanted what others seemed to have, yet at the same time you felt rage toward what they had. (Just as hatred is the shadow side of love, Envy, the vice of type Four is simply anger directed toward a *desired but unavailable* object.) Accordingly, you found yourself both wanting *and* hating what you were missing. As a result, you found that even when you could somehow manage to get some of it for yourself, you no longer wanted it. The traditional name for this state of mind is ego-melancholy. There is a French poem by Rainer Maria Rilke entitled "The Child at the Window" that gives a poignant sense of this state of melancholy and of how it affects one's perception:

> The child at the window awaits his mother's return.
> It has become that slow time of day
> when his very being is strained by endless waiting . . .
>
> And how will his soft shy glance ever find enough
> that everywhere sees only what is not enough
> to replace her matchless motherhood?
>
> These hazy passers-by flattened by his watch,
> tell me, are they at fault for not being her
> who alone seems enough . . . ?

R.M. Rilke, *L'enfant à la Fenêtre*, translated by W. Schafer. The original French is reprinted below:

> *L'enfant, à la fenêtre, attend le retour de sa mère.*
> *C'est l'heure lente où son être s'altère*
> *d'attente illimitée . . . .*
>
> *Comment suffire à son doux regard préliminaire*
> *qui partout ne voit que ce qui diffère*
> *de l'unique maternité?*
>
> *Ces vagues passantes que son attente nivelle*
> *ont-ils tort, dites, de ne pas être celle*
> *qui tant suffit . . . ?*

The state of ego-melancholy—a state of "sweet" but unquenchable longing—is a false substitute for the intuition of one's original connection to the divine that was lost in infancy. But once it becomes the core of the Four's egoic identity, it begins to be sought after for its own sake. And when feelings become the psyche's innermost reality (more accurately, when the soul identifies as feelings), a person naturally begins to seek more and more intense emotion in order to feel more "real." The life of a Four running on ego power then turns into a roller coaster of emotional highs and lows. Appreciation for the individual landscape of each hill and valley gets lost in the drama of sharp ascents and sudden plunges. The actual experience of each emotion is eclipsed by the excitement of the ride itself. Superficially, the drama of it all makes Fours feel alive and passionate. At a deeper level, however, the drama appears to be a subtle version of the collapse into inertia experienced by types Nine and Five. Although Fours outwardly appear to be highly emotional, in truth, they often have a hard time finding their own deepest feelings. Like Nines who can't set their own course, Fours can't quite locate their own personal desires. Instead they seem to absorb other people's feelings just like Nines who so easily take on other people's agendas. And finally, like Nines who can't easily change course once they have been given one, when Fours absorb a feeling, particularly a negative one, the emotion seems to take over and start running on its own. It doesn't matter that the emotion is not the Four's feeling but somebody else's. Once it starts to rev up, the Four seems unable to tune it out.

Point of Avoidance, Virtue, and Vice of Type Four

Fours experience a keen sense of searching for what is authentic, unique, and individual. This is how they attempt to re-establish their lost connection to Origin, which is the direct awareness of being an authentic and unique expression of the Divine. But this awareness has been disconnected from its essential energy. The ego does not know how to live authentically all on its own. The only way back to the Source is to give up the dramatic search outside of oneself for what seems to be missing and to look for it quietly within. At first this will seem foolish. Why look for something in a place one cannot recall ever having seen it? Just below that thought lies an even greater hesitation.

Searching within the self will bring up the fear of uncovering a great void within. Better the drama of great suffering than the quiet shame of feeling deficient.

The virtue traditionally associated with type Four is called Equanimity. It is the realization that life can be deeply meaningful without roller coasters. It requires the willingness to experience, not just the highs and lows, but the in-betweens, as well. Here is where the Four's point of avoidance comes into play. The point of avoidance of type Four is called Ordinary Living. Ordinary seems flat; it lacks envy's angry negation of desire. In the initial stages of spiritual work, the Four will be tempted to feel that trading in the passion of envy for the virtue of equanimity would be selling out one's deepest energy in order to buy mediocrity. The hesitation is somewhat justified if equanimity only means going along with others and keeping a flat-line emotional profile. The tendency to confuse equanimity with ordinariness is probably the most common obstacle to spiritual growth encountered by Fours.

Pivot of Dao for Type Four

But what if equanimity is experienced within the Pivot of Dao? The *daoshu* is not just a midway point between two extremes, a kind of compromise between too much and not enough. It is a true zero point, empty, still, and endlessly creative. It is the place from which the Four's inner emptiness is transformed into a container capable of holding the Limitless. The difficulty most Fours have entering the Pivot of Dao is that they seem to encounter small and medium-sized ego attacks so rarely. For most people it is easier to remain still when pain of type has been activated if the pain is still relatively small. Fours are not easily convinced that their suffering might be small! And obviously, it is harder to remain still in the face of a dire emergency. So what is a Four to do?

Let us suppose you encounter a situation in which you feel unnoticed or worse yet, disrespected (a not uncommon situation for many Fours). Left to itself, the feeling will simply grow larger until it becomes unbearable. When this happens it is helpful to remind yourself as early as you can: "This feels like a huge blow, but I know from past experience that it will eventually become more manageable."

Ask yourself, "Do I need to let these feelings run their full gamut right now, or might there be some benefit to moving into my head and thinking about the situation rather than just feeling it?" For most heart types becoming the observer feels a little like moving up into the head. The pivot of Dao is slightly more accessible from there. (This is not always the case for head types, who are identified with their thoughts in the first place.) If you can simply observe the size of the emotional storm battering your ego without getting caught up in the story behind the storm, the size itself will begin to suggest something else. That something else is the size of your consciousness, which is infinite. This is how the excessive *yin* energy ("I am overwhelmed") begins to shift toward more balance with *yang* ("I am formless awareness welcoming the drama of human life").

The following poem was written by Tagore upon the death of his mother. It powerfully describes the process by which the hole that loss augers out within the heart is transformed into an immense vessel of love:

> In desperate hope I go and search for her in all the corners of my room; I find her not.
>
> My house is small and what once has gone from it can never be regained.
>
> But infinite is thy mansion, my lord, and seeking her I have come to thy door.
>
> I stand under the golden canopy of thine evening sky and lift my eager eyes to thy face.
>
> I have come to the brink of eternity from which nothing can vanish – no hope, no happiness, no vision of a face seen through tears.
>
> Oh, dip my emptied life into that ocean, plunge it into the deepest fullness. Let me for once feel that lost sweet touch in the allness of the universe.

Rabindranath Tagore, *Gitanjali*, No. 87

The initial house of the ego is so small that it can never recover from its losses. But the seeking and searching itself leads to a doorway to the infinite. From that threshold, one falls into a space so vast nothing can ever disappear from it. This is the transformation possible if one is willing to remain at what is called "the point of rest on the potter's wheel of Heaven." It is the Daoist version of the *axis mundi* (center of the earth) in which the ego's division of the myriad things into good/bad, right/wrong, self/other, and even finite/infinite is transcended. As Fours explore this pivot, energies shift slightly and they can start surrendering their automatic attraction to the roller coaster for something better: exploring the expansive, irrepressible authenticity which lies at the heart of each ordinary encounter with life. To experience this is to come into contact with the "allness" of the universe, that is, to live in awareness of Holy Origin.

TYPE SEVEN

Holy Ideas: Work, Plan, Wisdom

Enneatype Seven, a mental type, is unbalanced toward *yang* energy. Three names are traditionally associated with its Holy Idea. The first is Holy Work. The meaning here is not work as in "labor," but work as in the phrase "a work of art." The second term, Holy Plan, emphasizes the fact that this work of art is intelligent rather than machinelike. This does not mean "plan" in the sense of predetermined plot, however. As any artist will tell you, a masterpiece does not begin with a blueprint fully formed in the artist's mind. I once asked a master weaver, "When you begin a piece, where is the design, in your head or on the loom?" He answered, "When I start I have the seed of an idea, but the loom and I have to solve its working out between us."

Taken together, these two Holy Ideas refer to an awareness of how life brilliantly creates beautiful patterns. Remember, Sevens are fueled by an abundance of creative and expansive *yang* energy. The following poem of Rabindranath Tagore describes the world seen through the lens of such dazzling and dancing energy. Read it out loud, remembering again how his poems are actually songs, and feel how it moves:

> Light, my light, the world-filling light, the eye-kissing light, heart-sweetening light!
>
> Ah, the light dances, my darling, at the centre of my life; the light strikes, my darling, the chords of my love; the sky opens, the wind runs wild, laughter passes over the earth.
>
> The butterflies spread their sails on the sea of light. Lilies and jasmines surge up on the crest of the waves of light.
>
> The light is shattered into gold on every cloud, my darling, and it scatters gems in profusion.
>
> Mirth spreads from leaf to leaf, my darling, and gladness without measure. The heaven's river has drowned its banks and the flood of joy is abroad.

Rabindranath Tagore, *Gitanjali*, No. 57

Lastly, Holy Wisdom refers to the psychological effect of perceiving Holy Work and Plan—namely the ability to align oneself with life's unfolding rather than the compulsion to continually devise schemes to get the result one craves. The term wisdom reminds us that Sevens are mental types who process experience primarily by thinking. Hence Holy Wisdom also refers to the perception of how Being evolves according to a fundamental intelligence. Sevens are particularly alive to this structure of life's unfolding, awareness of which can be likened to beholding a waterfall. At each moment, new water falls over the ledge, but the waterfall itself is continuous. From the point of view of the ego, we seem to live in a world of stable entities enduring through unidirectional time. From the point of view of essence, however, the world is continually arising new within one unchanging eternal now.

Initial Wounding and Subsequent Development of Type Seven

More than any other type, Sevens are alive to the mysterious unfolding of the timeless Dao manifesting as physical world developing in time. As newborns they first lived in "real time," that is they abided in presence to the flow of Be-ing. But their environment couldn't hold them there. No matter how attentive and caring their parents were, their infant souls experienced moments of disorganization. To use the phrase of David Winnicot, a British psychoanalyst who helped pioneer the modern study of infancy, they underwent a series of "annihilations." Their parents could not help them regain a sense of ongoingness within vital energy as the parents had lost their own ability to abide within it. Eventually, young Sevens lost awareness of *yang's* natural rhythms. The resulting sense of disorientation became the knothole around which their personality crystallized.

As a child, each Seven tried to recreate the lost connection to the "light dancing at the centre of my life" by mentally moving outward, mapping and planning for the future. This distortion of their natural *yang* creativity, nurtured within a mental environment, resulted in a personality style given to compulsive planning and scheming. Life became a continual preoccupation with the question, "What's next?" It was the only substitute they could devise for their lost sense of being in the midst of dancing light scattering gold on every cloud.

Underneath this mental preoccupation was an emotional pain. When contact with heaven's river was lost, the joy went out of living. The emotional landscape became parched, and young Sevens began to experience a longing for Paradise Lost. So they taught themselves how to avoid boredom and pain and search for pleasure instead. This marked the final distortion of their original *yang* energy. Recall how the *yang* energy of types Three and Eight overflows into unrestrained excess when it grows unbalanced. In a similar manner, the unbalanced energy of a Seven turns into unbridled mental scheming about avoiding any form of boredom, limitation, or pain and searching for every possible opportunity for diversion, novelty, and pleasure. This unquenchable hunger is the root of Enneatype Seven's passion, which is called Gluttony.

Point of Avoidance, Virtue and Vice of Type Seven

The spiritual path for Sevens calls for the virtue of Constancy. Ichazo defines it as "the state of [being] firmly grounded in the moment, taking in no more and no less than [needed], expending precisely as much energy as necessary." Its cultivation requires that Sevens voluntarily stay present to pleasure *and* pain, excitement *and* boredom, growth *and* decay. This is difficult, given that their point of avoidance is precisely pain and boredom. Just like Fours who can easily believe that ordinary living is a bad trade-off for giving up envy, Sevens initially feel that constancy is a dreary substitute for gluttony. They feel like heavy smokers who have been told "quit or die." Immediately they want to reply, "But then there is no point to living!"

Pivot of Dao for Type Seven

With each Enneatype, I have been attempting to illuminate the notion of the Pivot of Dao further. There is a short teaching story at the end of chapter 2 of the *Zhuangzi* that may help us continue that process as we consider type Seven's dilemma:

> Previously, Zhuang Zhou dreamt he had become a carefree butterfly, a happy flittering butterfly, who himself experienced such a fit between his intents and his surroundings, that he didn't know he was Zhou.
> Suddenly he awoke, and was unmistakably, undeniably Zhou.
> He didn't know if he was Zhou who had dreamt he had been a carefree butterfly, or a carefree butterfly dreaming that he had become Zhou.
> Between Zhou and the carefree butterfly there must be a distinction!
> This is called "the transformation of things."[8]

The carefree butterfly is the Seven, running happily along on ego power. For the moment, it seems possible to spend one's life having fun, seeking pleasure, thinking always of tomorrow. Then comes the wake up call. Some type of set-back abruptly interrupts the "dream" and the Seven is face to face with pain, loss, boredom, and ultimately death. The jarring ring of the alarm is unmistakable, undeniable. In the aftermath of the shock, a doubt arises: Can I continue flittering like a carefree butterfly, or must I endure everyday humdrum life instead? The doubt represents the beginning of Zhou's real awakening, for he has begun to question his egoic identity. But he hasn't resolved the doubt yet, for the two alternatives still seem mutually exclusive. Either he remains a flittering butterfly trying to force a perfect "fit" between his wants and his experience, or he has to be dull, bored, and suffering Zhou.

---

8 I am indebted for both the translation of this passage and for the seeds of the following interpretation to Lusthaus, 2003.

At first the story appears to say that one cannot be sure whether one is Zhou or the butterfly. Closer reading shows that this is not the case. The butterfly has no awareness of Zhou, but Zhou remembers the butterfly. Zhou the story-teller has no doubts about who really had the dream. It is only the butterfly who is truly asleep. The Zhou who doubts his own reality is, in fact, awakening, for he finds himself in the transition state between ego and enlightened wakefulness. For the moment, neither is clear, but there is nonetheless a subjective certainty that there *must* be a solution. The solution can be reached only by entering the Pivot of Dao where an entirely new vision appears precisely because all resistance has been dropped. Daoists call this the transformation of things. The "real" Zhou, located within the Internal Observer, resides in the still center of what *Zhuangzi* in other places calls "the potter's wheel of heaven." He is aware that at the deepest level that he is neither butterfly nor ordinary Zhou but an instance of still consciousness that is aware of being both at once.

Being both at once. This is a key realization, not just for Sevens but for all types. From the point of view of the observer, both realities are equally so. I am a human being, and therefore I have this history and this personality. I am from time to time identified with it. That is, I think that this is all that I am. Hence I suffer. I am also infinite awareness, consciousness itself. From time to time I catch glimpses of that, as well. This brings me great bliss. Between the two states is a huge tension. The tension is my cross, stretching me from one world into the other. Like Jesus I can cry out, "I thirst." And like him I can say, "Not my will but yours"—not following my ego's plan but allowing the holy weaving of my life to work itself out between me and this all-wise loom.

If Sevens will tolerate the tension of these transitional states long enough, they will gradually notice a transformation. Their energy will shift from unrestrained driving to finding the next interesting option to a more balanced appreciation for the underdetermined surprises and delights awaiting discovery in every event gushing forth from the eternal spring of the present moment. Gradually, they will begin to sense how pleasure shifts from the act of mental mapping (an action that is overly *yang*) to the experience of enjoying the surprise of the moment (which implies a balance with *yin* receptivity). This is the real meaning of Equanimity. With it a different kind of joyfulness can be experienced; one that comes naturally from within rather than being extorted from the environment. When the mind stops churning, it has the power to actually see into things. It sees how they are born, what sustains them, what injures them, how it is that they die, and what becomes of them then. The process itself becomes a source of delight. But the mind must first stop spinning. The *Nei-yeh* (Inward Training), an early Daoist text on meditation, asks what it means to be released by the Way. It replies:

> The answer resides in the calmness of the mind.
> When your mind is well ordered, your senses are well ordered.
> When your mind is calm, your senses are calmed.

A few lines further on it describes what awaits the seeker when the mind becomes calm:

> Within the mind there is yet another mind.
> That mind within the mind: it is an awareness that precedes words.

This is the awareness of the numinous mind, the experience of "I", of essence itself. Essence is not identified with either the structure of type or with the individual struggling to get free of type. It is simply aware. When Sevens are aware in this way, their consciousness becomes the light of Holy Work, Plan, and Wisdom dancing at the center of their life.

TYPE ONE

Holy Idea: Perfection

Enneatype One is the body triad's version of a type unbalanced toward the reconciling aspect of energy. The Holy Idea of type One is called Perfection. It is difficult to feel one's way into this particular Idea because all of our past conditioning about perfection causes us to understand it as a judgment based upon comparisons to some external standard. The aspect of Essence under consideration here, however, is neither mental nor has anything to do with comparisons or standards. Holy Perfection refers to Being's completeness of *be-ing*. The Latin root from which this word is derived is *perficere*. It is composed of the preposition *per* (through) and the verb stem *facere* (to make). Perfection refers to the fact that something is *completely* and *wholly* what it is. It has been "made all the way through." All of Being has a quality of fundamental faultlessness just because it *is wholly as it is*. The Holy Idea of Perfection is the intuition of this central aspect of Being's "as-it-is-ness." Daoists call this *ziran*. *Ziran* is the power of each being to spontaneously "self-so."

There is a marvelous poem of Gerard Manley Hopkins that (perfectly!) captures the meaning of *ziran*. It is titled "Kingfishers Catch Fire." The first eight lines simply ring with the feeling of how each thing explodes into its own being. The final six lines then portray Hopkins' Christian understanding of what it means to live in the awareness of this "graced" aspect of original energy. This is a poem that truly needs to be read aloud—almost shouted out loud—in order to be appreciated:

As kingfishers catch fire, dragonflies draw flame;
As tumbled over rim in roundy wells
Stones ring; like each tucked string tells, each hung bell's
Bow swung finds tongue to fling out broad its name;

Each mortal thing does one thing and the same:
Deals out that being indoors each one dwells;
Selves—goes itself; *myself* it speaks and spells,
Crying *What I do is me: for that I came.*

I say more: the just man justices;
Keeps grace: that keeps all his goings graces;
Acts in God's eye what in God's eye he is—

Christ—for Christ plays in ten thousand places,
Lovely in limbs, and lovely in eyes not his
To the Father through the features of men's faces.

G.M. Hopkins, *Wessex Poems*, 1918

Initial Wounding and Subsequent Development of Type One

Type One is particularly drawn to the reconciling aspect of energy, a tendency it shares with types Six and Two. This makes Ones especially sensitive to *yin* and *yang's* endless play and to any appearance of tension between them. They experience all of this in a visceral manner since as body types their perceptions are processed kinesthetically. Originally, the experience is a pervading sense of bliss over how each mortal being "deals out that being indoors each one dwells." But embodiment threatens the One's capacity to maintain such awareness, and eventually the One's flowing energy begins to collapse. As Ones lose their sense that reality is fundamentally "self-so," their awareness begins to narrow. The loss of Essence feels like a wave of wrongness. The wave then intensifies. Badness seems everywhere, within the self and without, and the narrowness of vision seems only to increase its intensity. The resulting knothole is called Anger, which is the passion or vice of type One. Anger is defined by Ichazo as a "stand against reality the way it is." It resides in the belly of the One as a kind of a cosmic sense that God goofed. The consequent fault-finding relationship to the world thus becomes the One's first distortion of original energy. Around this knothole of anger the ego of the One begins to crystallize.

As children, Ones learned to convert their lost sense of perfection into a type of inner effort called "improving." They kept trying to get it right, to *re*-create perfection. But all their efforts only took them away from their own instinctual energy. As body types, they came to sense the body itself as a central focal point for wrongness. And with the loss of access to instinctual energy they lost the internal yardstick for evaluating life. External yardsticks then had to be found. They became preoccupied with rules[9] and began a lifetime of striving to correct both themselves and those around them. A counterfeit version of the spontaneous experience of *ziran* was created. It was called "correctness." The need to correct self and everyone else felt like a rush of urgency experienced in a visceral way (even though many of those around them may have seen them as mental types). The urge to correct what is wrong

9 Rules are to the One what authority is for the Six—substitutes for inner knowing.

then became the final distortion of their original reconciling energy. Instead of seeking balance, they grew narrow-minded and rigid, seeing only what was wrong and remaining blind to everything else.

Of course, underneath the conscious urge to correct was a deep well of anger. The rage collected because when Ones lose touch with instinctual energy, they also lose joy. The zest of being alive in a world that "keeps grace" disappears. No wonder they are angry! But since anger is not a "correct" emotion it has to be concealed. The cruel trap that squeezes Ones between anger over perceived imperfection and the prohibition to be angry forces the final collapse of their original balanced energy into tightness and rigidity. Crueler yet, the anger can never be completely suppressed because giving up anger seems tantamount to acquiescing to reality's badness. Egoic life as a One becomes a tightly constricted knot of anger trying to hold down anger.

Point of Avoidance, Virtue, and Vice of Type One

Type One is the only member of the Enneagram whose passion is identical to its point of avoidance. That combination erects a cruel cage indeed, and Ones possibly suffer more within its confines than any other type. It makes the spiritual path for Ones more than a little complicated. The practical problem for Ones often has to do with a basic misunderstanding of what drives the type. Ones are often tempted to think that they will improve if they simply relax their standards, making them more adaptive and in line with the standards of everyone else. This will bring only superficial change, however. The root problem of the fixation does not lie in having inflexible standards; it lies in placing one's hopes in standards in the first place. Standards belong to the domain of content, the world of form, the world of "me." Standards are always relative to some point of view. We can say that an expensive car is better than a cheap one. And from one point of view this is correct. The expensive car is likely to be larger, quieter, more comfortable, and more elegant. Yet from another point of view the cheap car could be considered better. It is likely to be smaller, more maneuverable, easier to park, and more fuel efficient. We could make a similar point about people, cultures, moral systems, or anything else one could think of. Standards are always relative to judgments about content. Only when one leaves the domain of content altogether and enters that of Being do standards disappear. From the perspective of Being, it can be seen that the root of the One fixation does not lie principally in the mind. The core of the fixation lies in an instinctive reaction—anger—to the fact that one is living an embodied existence. Ones are first and foremost body types.

The virtue for type One is called Serenity. Its practice, however, is not easy because in the early stages of spiritual work most Ones are tempted to believe that the virtue they need most is "improvement." Self-improvement is a poor substitute for serenity. Ones can torture themselves (and those around them) with judgments about progress and lack of progress. It is easy to forget that spiritual work can be intrinsically rewarding and full of humor. (There is an ancient Daoist saying: "The perfect path is effortless." Its message is especially difficult for Ones.) The One's automatic tendency is to fight anger with perfection (understood as improvement). Whenever anger arises, Ones feel that the situation has lurched too far toward *yang*. The anger simply feels too instinctual and out of control. They then want to apply more perfection, which they experience as forced compliance to standard. But such a remedy seems too passively *yin* and only creates more anger because the One's vital instincts to "self-so" run contrary to forced compliance. In the end, Ones feel trapped between *yang* (anger) and *yin* (compliance). In a manner reminiscent of what happens to types Six and Two when they begin to constrict, Ones tighten down, trying to assuage each *yang* impulse with an equal and opposite *yin* impulse, increasing the vibration of their egoic oscillation to an intolerable pitch.

The virtue of Serenity allows people to leave the maelstrom of perfectionism fighting anger altogether. They can stop fighting against and begin to drop straight down into their experience—even if it happens to be that of anger. In this regard, it is important for Ones to remember that Serenity does not mean passive compliance to the rules of good behavior. Neither does it mean that a person simply gives in to rage. It does not even mean that a person just says and does nothing when angry. Serenity, experienced within the Pivot of Dao, manages to turn the table on the whole cruel game of perfection vs. anger. True serenity (from the Latin *serenus*—"clear, unclouded") implies clear vision. It means that one sees all the way through the situation and perceives how each element (*de*) of it "selves" as a manifestation of *Dao*.

Pivot of Dao for Type One

How does such a transformation occur for type One? As there was for Zhou, there must be a distinction between the one who is angry and the one who is angry about being angry. And as for Zhou, the answer lies in the transition between being self-righteously angry (a butterfly whose world perfectly fits his view of it) and being hit with the unmistakable, undeniable evidence that he is Zhou (self-so, as-he-is, mourning the loss of Perfection). When you cease reacting against the anger—even the deep anger-against-reality-the-way-it-is—you begin to discover that below it lies grief, and below that, longing. The longing is for Perfection, your original state of joy about the world as it springs forth from its origin in divine consciousness. The grief is the lifetime you have spent pinched up and dissatisfied because you let go of that original state. When you let yourself be still and welcoming, however, the clear consciousness that identifies neither with rage nor with anger at the rage simply observes the deep hurt of one who longs so deeply for Perfection that he feels its absence "perfectly," all-the-way-through. Keeping this in mind, return once more to the last six lines of the Hopkins' poem found a few pages earlier:

> I say more: the just man justices;
> Keeps grace: that keeps all his goings graces;
> Acts in God's eye what in God's eye he is—
>
> Christ—for Christ plays in ten thousand places,
> Lovely in limbs, and lovely in eyes not his
> To the Father through the features of men's faces.

If you are not Christian, or if you once were and are now angry about it, please put aside for a moment whatever knee-jerk reaction you have to the word "Christ." Christ playing in ten thousand places is a spiritual perception that is quite similar to the intuition of *Dao* giving birth to the universe.[10] The man Jesus is called the Christ because he fully realized his divine nature and lived accordingly. That same divine nature "plays" in every human being, just as *Dao* breathes within each and every *de*. In Christian language, the just man "justices," that is he imbues everything he sees with the divine perfection he experiences existing within himself. He "keeps grace," that is he steadfastly receives every instance of life as a gift, therefore he perceives the loveliness of the divine in the features of each and every human face. This is true Serenity, true clearness of vision. It leads to a stance that, instead of rejecting reality as it is, welcomes all of it in full awareness of Holy Perfection.

10 The Chinese ideograph for the universe is "the ten thousand things," and Hopkins' choice of words here may not be just coincidence.

PART IV: THE COSMIC TREE

Exploring the Human Condition

Most people think of the Enneagram as a map of the individual psyche, but it can also be regarded as a map of the human condition. Accordingly, we now turn to considerations of the Enneagram as archetypal symbol. After a summary of what we have seen so far of the Enneagram's deep structure, we will consider how it mirrors the path of spiritual healing, not just for individuals caught up in type, but for humanity itself. The final chapter will then describe four central practical issues facing anyone who seriously takes up a path of spiritual transformation.

Chapter 7:

The Enneagram as Archetypal Symbol

Summary of Types and Triangles

Each Enneatype appears to represent the conjunction of one aspect of universal energy with one specific center of experience. The defining characteristics of individual types appear to depend to a great extent upon the combination of the type's specific energetic imbalance and the predominant center of awareness used to process that energy. For example, unbalanced *yin* energy in a type that processes information viscerally yields type Nine's habit of merging with other people's plans and agendas. However, that same *yin* energy in a heart type produces the Four's tendency to absorb others' feelings, while in a mental type it results in Enneatype Five's inner drive to soak up knowledge.

A similar pattern can be seen among the *yang* types. Processed through an emotional center of experience, unbalanced *yang* energy manifests as the Three's habitual optimism and energy for doing. In the visceral center, it shows up as the Eight's full-power ahead excess. Finally, in the mental center, that same energy is poured into the Seven's habit of planning for the future.

Finally, the same pattern is found among types whose lack of balance has to do with the reconciling aspect of energy. In a mental type, unbalanced reconciling energy leads to Enneatype Six's preoccupation with security through analysis. In a body type, it results in Enneatype One's preoccupation with what is wrong and how to correct it, and in an emotional type it produces Enneatype Two's preoccupation with egoism and altruism.

The resulting overall pattern is such that each fundamental aspect of universal energy can be found once within each center of intelligence. Among the body triad, Eight is *yang*, Nine is *yin*, and One is reconciling. Within emotional types there is a *yang* member (Three), a *yin* member (Four) and a reconciling member (Two). Among the mental types, Seven is *yang*, Five is *yin*, and Six is reconciling. For your convenience, Figure 4 has been reproduced once more:

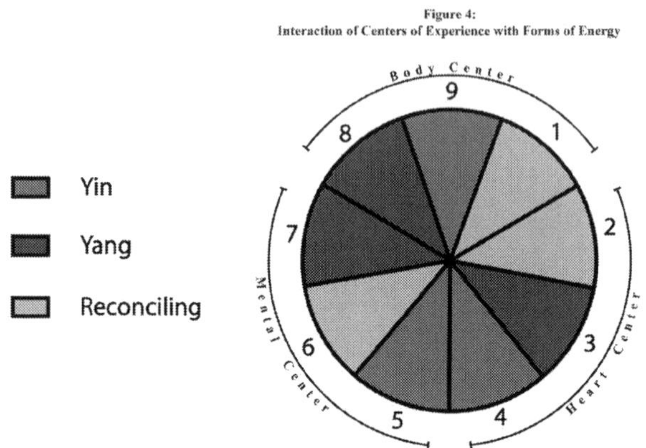

Each of the three aspects of life energy has its own manner of undergoing distortion as the ego develops. The original energy with which we are born is free flowing and balanced. It is open to all experience. As *yin*, it flows inward as openness, but it can also flow outward as flexibility of action. When *yin* becomes constricted, both flows are stifled, resulting in inertia and a concern with boundaries. Depending upon which center of intelligence is involved, the inertia and boundary concerns are expressed primarily in the behavioral, emotional, or mental arenas. Nines fear boundaries because they are so receptive, for boundaries threaten them with separation. Fours and Fives, again because they are so receptive, find it hard to set up sufficient boundaries to keep others' feelings or demands from overwhelming them.

Balanced *yang* energy engages with life in a multiplicity of ways. It can either lead to decisive action or alert stillness. When unbalanced, however, it reacts by overflowing in an unrestrained fashion. The overflow is then expressed primarily in behavioral, emotional, or mental ways, again depending up which center of intelligence is involved. As heart types, Threes seek emotional connection to the world through compulsive production of success. Sevens (mental types) compulsively plan and live in a world of magical tomorrow, whereas body center Eights compulsively seek stimulation and excitement.

Lastly, balanced reconciling energy is simply the natural equilibrium of *yin* and *yang*. But when egoic efforts to over-control the balance disrupt the natural balance, the energy collapses into a narrow and amplifying rigidity, either behaviorally, emotionally, or mentally. Sixes focus narrowly on the potential for danger and intensify its significance. Twos focus narrowly on what the special someone needs to be given and intensify the gift's importance to that person. Ones focus narrowly on standards of right and wrong and magnify their importance in the grand scheme of life. The end resulting pattern is that of nine different energy distortions, briefly summarized in Table 3.

Table 3: The Fundamental Energies and Their Distortions

Enneatype	Experience Center	Flowing Energy	"Stuck" Energy (Inertia/Overflow/Narrowing-Intensification)
		YIN TYPES	
Nine	Belly	Absorbing	Behavioral Inertia (can't choose own agenda/ can't shift course once set)
Four	Heart	Absorbing	Emotional Inertia (absorbs others' feelings/ gets stuck in own feelings)
Five	Head	Absorbing	Mental Inertia (stingy about revealing/ clings to knowledge)
		YANG TYPES	
Three	Heart	Expanding	Emotional Overflow (compulsive production of successful image)
Seven	Head	Expanding	Mental Overflow (compulsive planning of pleasant options)
Eight	Belly	Expanding	Behavioral Overflow (compulsive excess of just about everything)
		RECONCILING TYPES	
Six	Head	Reconciling	Mental Narrowing/ Intensification (narrow focus on dangers/strategies for security)
One	Belly	Reconciling	Behavioral Narrowing/ Intensification (rigid urgency about one correct way)
Two	Heart	Reconciling	Emotional Narrowing/ Intensification (intense preoccupation with others' needs while magnifying importance of self)

The Traditional and Equilateral Triangle Models of the Enneagram

Contemplated this way, the nine types are distributed around the circle of the Enneagram in three equilateral triangles. Those of you who have studied the Enneagram elsewhere know that this is not the traditional way the Enneagram is presented. The traditional model places types Nine, Three and Six on an equilateral triangle but arranges the remaining types along an irregular hexagon formed by types One, Four, Two, Eight, Five and Seven. You may recall how it looks from Figure 1, first found in Chapter 1.

Figure 1:
The Enneagram Symbol

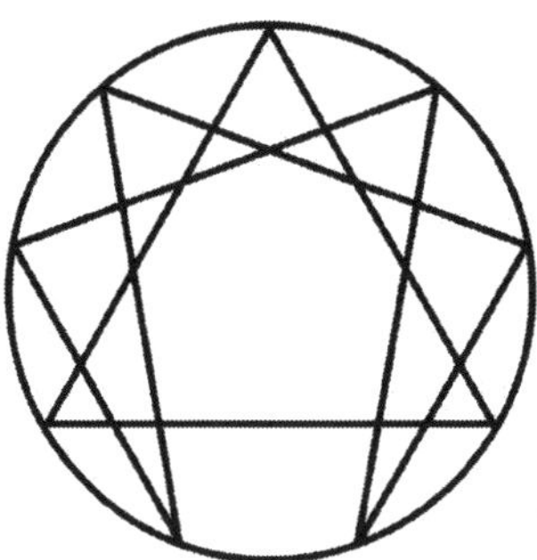

The model offered in this book is slightly different and looks like Figure 11:

Figure 11:
The Equilateral Triangle Model of the Enneagram

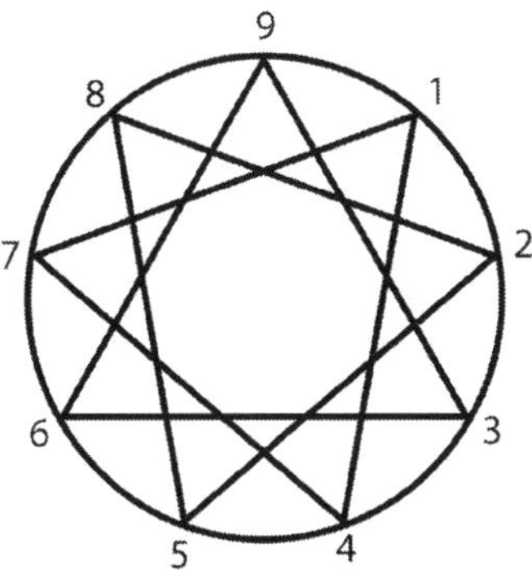

I am not proposing that the traditional model is wrong. It is based upon an ancient understanding called the law of Seven and has provided powerful insights about spiritual development to innumerable students, myself included. However, the arrangement of types offered in this book[11] yields several worthwhile advantages that complement the original study. One has already been mentioned, namely that in this arrangement all triangles are isomorphic. Within each triangle is one example of each center of awareness and one example of each aspect of original energy. The second advantage has to do with a discussion of Enneagram theory, which has been tabled until now. I am referring to that part of the theory that talks about each type's points of stress and security.

Movement toward Security and Stress or toward Balance?

If one inspects the nine-pointed star of the Enneagram (either the traditional drawing or the one used here), it is obvious that each type is connected to two other types by lines drawn between them. These lines are not drawn just to embellish the design; they have a purpose. For example, as a Six, I have one line to type Three and a second line to type Nine. These two types are often called my points of stress (Three) and security (Nine).[12] In the model I am presenting, some of the stress and security points change. In the traditional model, type Two is connected to Eight, a body type, and also to Four, which is another heart type. Hence it has no connection to a mental type. Similarly, type Seven is connected to One, a body type, and to Five, another mental type. Again, there is no connection to any heart type. This means that in the traditional model, types Two and Four lack "legs" to a mental type whereas types Five and Seven lack them to a heart type. In the model I

---

11 The design is not original, in that I do not claim to have invented it. It can be found in the place of the more traditional design in many ancient references.

12 Clockwise movement around the triangle is considered movement toward security and counterclockwise movement toward stress. Thus for type Nine, the point of security is Three and that of stress is Six. In the traditional model, the types on the hexagon move toward security in the direction of One, Seven, Five, Eight, Two, Four and back to One. The opposite direction is called movement toward stress.

am offering here, this situation is remedied. Type Two is connected to Five, and type Four is connected to Seven. Hence, Two and Four, both heart types, each have a line to a mental type as well as to a body type. Similarly, mental types Five and Seven have lines connecting them to heart types (Two and Four), whereas before they were connected to one another as reciprocal points of stress and security. In the model offered here, every type is connected to a type of each of the other two centers of experience. Each type is also connected to a type that predominantly uses one of the other two aspects of life energy. This brings a greater sense of balance to the distribution of stress and security points for all types.

The entire discussion about stress and security in Enneagram teaching has to my mind delivered some benefit but at the cost of considerable confusion. The basic problem is that the choice of terms like security and stress immediately makes everyone suppose that movement toward security is good and movement toward stress is bad. For instance, the point of stress for Eights is Five, and the point of security is Two. This is often taken to mean that Eights are supposed to be developing toward Two and not toward Five. The argument goes something like this. Under stress, Eights go inward like Fives, stop communicating, obsess over things, and generally implode, but in security, they move toward others just like Twos and harness their considerable energy to be of service. It sounds convincing at first. But many Eights under stress do not go inward. They become even more externally oriented and move "toward" others by bossing them around or even abusing them. And when secure, many Eights are able to halt the excessive activity and take some pleasure from their own curiosity to know Truth more deeply. The fact of the matter seems to be that any type has much to learn from either of its allied points and that growth is more a matter of balance than of movement in one direction only. Hence it seems sensible to simply jettison the vocabulary of stress vs. security altogether. It would be clearer if we called the other two types that lie on our own triangle our *points of balance*, for they offer the possibility of bringing greater balance, not only to our manner of processing experience, but also to the aspects of life energy that we use in the process.

I hope that by now I have convinced you that it is too literal-minded and limiting to require that individual types "move" only in certain directions. Fives on a growth path should not try to look more and more like Eights, nor should they shy away from the qualities of Twos. A Five whose energy is greatly unbalanced can appear quite arrogant (Eight-like) as well as resentful (Two-like). However, a Five who is living in the free flow of his or her original energy is naturally going to be more actively engaged in practical affairs (like Eights), as well as more generous and concerned with service (like Twos). The key to growth is entry into the resistance-free point of the *daoshu* and recovery of one's Holy Idea. This will automatically bring into play the Holy Ideas of the two types on the same triangle. In spiritual work, stillness works better than trying to focus one's movement in a certain direction. The types on each triangle appear to offer one another certain possibilities for either growth or deterioration simply because the triangle as a whole contains the balance of life force energies and modes of awareness specific to the basic developmental focus of the triangle.

Kinship of Types within Triangles

The final advantage of the model put forward here is that each triangle has certain overall characteristics that give its three types a certain feeling of commonality. People who find themselves in any one triangle generally feel a certain familiarity with the other two types of their triangle. For example, as a Six, I recognize Threes and Nines as types having much in common with me, even though I am not exactly like them. They feel kind of like cousins, in that they don't live quite the way I do, but because I visit them with some frequency, I find their ways familiar. In my teaching, I have found many students who share this same sense of familiarity with those on their triangle.[13] For example, most Fours recognize that they can easily become quite critical, sometimes sounding like Ones. According to traditional Enneagram

13 I have found that it is often helpful to keep this in mind when interviewing people in order to help them find their type. For example, when trying to help someone decide whether he or she is a Nine or a Four, it can be useful to hear whether they resonate more to types Three and Six, or to types Seven and One.

teaching, this is quite predictable, for type Four has a connection to type One (its so-called point of security). But in the traditional model, Four's other connection is to type Two. While it is true that many Fours recognize that they sometimes feel pressed to behave a little like Twos (their supposed point of stress), my conversations with them indicate that they are even more accustomed to experiencing either the creative originality or the anxious disorientation typical of Sevens, who are fellow members of their triangle in the model I have presented here.

A Triangle of Triangles

Each triangle symbolizes different aspects of a certain stage of the drama of humanity's spiritual quest. All three triangles together portray how the stages themselves form a directional unity throughout the entire quest

The Earth Triangle

I think of the triangle formed by types Nine, Six, and Three as the Earth Triangle. In Chinese cosmology, Earth *Qi* is another designation for *jing*, or vital quintessence. *Jing* is life force in the process of moving from the unmanifest world to the manifest world. It is the energy that guides the basic process of incarnation. Held primarily in the lower *dan tian*, it governs our concrete physical and sexual existence. Earth Triangle therefore seems the term best suited to convey how the three types of the central triangle portray at a cosmic level the drama of incarnation. Individuals of these three types share a certain deep preoccupation with the predicament of embodied existence. Types Nine, Three, and Six are archetypes of the three shocks of embodiment—the Loss of Wholeness (Nine), the Loss of Emotional Connection to Source (Three) and the Loss of Trust (Six). If we examine the three types in the counterclockwise direction the triangle can be taken as a map of the developmental stages of the soul's fall from essence. I am referring, of course, to the infant's sequential discoveries that life as a body is uncomfortable (beginning with birth), that it is moreover dangerous due to parental failure to protect (beginning with the first year of life), and finally that one's true nature is invisible to others (most characteristically, in the second and third years of life).

When read in the opposite direction, however, the path of Nine to Three to Six to Nine again can be viewed as a description of the human spiritual journey. It begins with the soul's initial merger with essence (Nine), continues with its individuation into a human ego or personality (Three) whose consciousness is gradually transformed into the awareness that it is both human individual *and* embodiment of divine spirit (Six), and finally returns to merger with essence again (Nine). The first direction describes what Sandra Maitri has called the "logic of the soul" as it unravels into egoic type. The second direction could be called the Path of Essence, for it nicely conveys the energic movement of spiritual growth.

We can also approach the spiritual meaning the central triangle of types in another manner. The three Holy Ideas of the Enneagram's central triangle of Love, Hope, and Faith (the three so-called "theological" virtues of Christianity) stand to one another in the following way. Love is the universal acceptance of all being just as it is; Hope is the creative wave of its natural unfolding; and Faith is the abiding trust that these two are in complete harmony with each other. You will find a quite similar notion embedded in the title of the most famous text of Daoism, attributed to Laozi. The *Daodejing* is a book that describes how formless presence (*dao*) unfolds into each individual identity (*de*) in such a way that both together form one harmonious relationship (*jing*).[14]

The Human Triangle

Rotated slightly counterclockwise from the central triangle is a second equilateral triangle formed by types Five, Eight, and Two. I call this the Human Triangle. In Daoist thought, human *qi* represents the inner, personal aspect of the life force and is said to reside primarily in the heart center. At a societal level, the three types of this triangle share

14 The term *jing* in this text is not identical to the term *jing* used earlier to mean vital quintessence. The apparent confusion arises because Chinese is a tonal language and what looks like the same phoneme when written in Roman characters can have different meanings depending upon how it is inflected.

the basic tasks of humanizing embodied animal life: the development of science, politics, and service. If we follow the clockwise direction of the Path of Essence, we find that type Five is an archetype of the quest for understanding and wisdom, which when sought from the point of view of essence rather than ego produces concrete benefits for the entire community. Type Eight moving innocently in essence rather than making war in egoic fashion, mobilizes this wisdom and organizes it in order to build and defend a just society. Type Two when connected to its original energy permeates that society with a genuine concern for service to all other forms of life without selfish overlays of intrusion or control. In this manner we see that the Human Triangle's Holy Ideas form a map for the creation of an enlightened human society. Omniscience generates Truth which leads to true Freedom.

However, if we imagine the same triangle moving in the opposite direction, we find a path of social destruction. In terrifyingly modern fashion, the cycle describes a society whose members so fear the needs and claims of others (Five) that they become preoccupied with false privileges and freedoms for themselves (Two) and when this fails to produce true happiness and security, react with a resentful rage that is blind to all consequences (Eight), provoking even greater attacks from the outside world (Five again).

The Heaven Triangle

Types Four, Seven and One comprise what I call the Heaven Triangle. The word *tian* in classic Chinese is usually translated as heaven, but it can also mean nature. In the Chinese cosmology, heaven is not a place in the sky to which dead people migrate. Instead it represents a state of affairs in which earth and humanity are in natural harmony. Heaven *qi*, gathered through the head center, is concerned with the numinous world of mystical experience, which is accessible when the energies of the two lower centers are in equilibrium. And indeed, the three types found on the Heaven Triangle each exhibit a strong sense of idealism and sensitivity to the creative and spiritual aspects of life. Viewed in this way the three types appear as archetypes of mystical development. The *yin* member, Four, when connected to essence, spontaneously recognizes the deeper significance of people and events and from that recognition supports their authentic self-expression. When aligned with original energy, the *yang* member Seven spontaneously radiates joy at the "self-so" beauty of each and every being. Finally, when Type One is connected to source, it immediately welcomes each being as an authentic self-expression of divine perfection. The three types, when seen in movement toward essence, thus represent a cycle of ever deepening spiritual awareness. Origin, the intuition of each being's roots in divine purpose, generates Wisdom, the awareness of life's evolution toward ever more marvelous wonders, which leads to Perfection, the perception of each being's self-so beauty as a work of divine creativity.

On the other hand, one could construct a path of spiritual decay for the triangle by moving in the opposite direction around the triangle. Lost connection to Origin (Four) prompts egoic effort to recreate Perfection as compliance to standard (One), which inevitably fails and in turn sets off a desperate search for distraction and pleasure (Seven) that only exacerbates the soul's sense of being cut off from its source (Four once more).

Finally, each triangle's own inner structure not only reveals different aspects of the life force's movement within distinct levels of the human drama, but the three triangles taken together symbolize the general evolution of consciousness itself. The Earth Triangle can be read as the story of spirit's devolution into matter, a process that implies both the creative movement of spirit's self-expression as material world and the fracturing movement of spirit's apparent individuation, differentiation, and separation within a material universe. It is the narrative of incarnation itself. The Human Triangle symbolizes the inborn tendency of physical beings, especially of the human kind, to join together and form individual, familial, and societal attachments as they seek to heal their painful sense of being separated from creative source. It tells the story of humanity's evolutionary movement toward greater understanding and deeper love. Finally, the Heaven Triangle stands for the final step of spirit's return to source as it achieves ever higher levels of consciousness and ever deepening levels of mystical experience.

In summary, the Enneagram's nine pointed star can be seen as a triangle of triangles that organizes into one dynamic whole qualities of being that span the entire gamut of human development: physical, social, and spiritual. As Almaas (1998) has pointed out, the Enneagram is like a jewel that reflects the whole spectrum of divine brilliance shimmering over the face of humanity. It is a truly cosmic symbol.

Conclusion: Symbolism and Types

As we close this summary chapter on Enneatypes, I want to reiterate that the Enneagram is more than a typology. A typology defines various categories. The Enneagram is a symbol of the process of spiritual evolution. Definitions and symbols are not the same. A definition puts an end to the conversation; a symbol begs it to continue. A definition is a wall; it says this far and no farther. A symbol is a window in the wall; it says stand in the right light, and I will show you your own features even as I open up to you a vision of what lies beyond. Definitions "explain" the world. Symbols "hide the world within the world." I hope by now it is clear to you that the Enneagram is a symbol, not a definition. It is far more than a list of nine categories or boxes into which we can put people. Nor is it a spiritual doctrine telling you to renounce your Ego in order to merge with Absolute Mind. It is a window that shows you your own human face even as it opens your heart and mind to a deeper vision of the cosmic reality in which you are a necessary and principal participant. It is a map of energy currents that flow through the universe, as well as through each individual. Almost all spiritual traditions share a certain double vision of reality, often aphoristically stated "as above, so below". The earth is a mirror of the heavens; the human body is a representation of the universe; the soul is poetry declaimed by a self-revealing deity. Seen in the light of the Enneagram, each human being is a microcosm of the energy that both emerges from and flows back toward the entire universe.

If I were a gifted graphic artist and this book were a computer screen, the diagrams of the Enneagram contained in it would be three-dimensional and alive with movement. Instead of black lines connecting nine types, they would have transparent channels in which energies of various colors surged both back and forth. Such a presentation might prevent you from misperceiving the Enneagram as a static definitional structure. But I would still want to warn you that the movement I have described in the preceding chapters should not be taken literally. The Enneagram is never literal, even as a description of movement. When I as a Six shift my energy toward Nine by opening myself and relaxing into the Pivot of Dao, I do not *become* a Nine. Fours do not become Sevens, then Ones, and so on and so on. As we relax into the full flow of *Dao*, we do not become new and different *de*, or condensation points within it. We remain who we are. As human beings, we are open to the possibilities of the infinite, but we still retain our unique destinies. The fundamental mystery of human existence is its paradoxical status as an integration of two realities, one finite and the other infinite. The integration is the ultimate mystery, for it is itself neither finite nor infinite. The Enneagram is a symbol in which we may contemplate but never define that mystery.

Chapter 8:

In the Shade of the Tree

This is the point at which I stop writing, and you begin practicing. Books can point to the path but only walking puts one on the path. These last pages are simply meant to highlight four central ideas or principles of spiritual work. Appendix A will suggest some initial practices in detail. If you want more than just beginning practices, you will do well find a teacher and a group to support your development.

Ugly Toads and Mushrooms

The first central principle has to do with the difference between the journey and the map. The Enneagram is not just a description of your type. It is a map that shows where to start undoing the spell type has cast. It leads to a gate, usually dark and cluttered with twisted thorny vines, called one's point of avoidance. Mircea Eliade (1959) reminds us that in most myths the hero's journey begins with an encounter with something astonishing—an ugly toad or mushroom, a slippery stairwell found in the fissure of a rock. Often the hero refuses the first invitation to enter. He would rather continue studying the map, hoping his destiny is to become a cartographer rather than an explorer. The astonishing occurrence has to visit him again and perhaps again. Remember this when great tragedy strikes your life. Remember it when you have to keep on living with an irritating boss or co-worker or family member. These are your ugly toads and mushrooms.

What makes one finally enter? Suffering, usually. It simply gets too painful to stay where you are. And if indeed you enter, you are then required to begin the solitary journey through the dark forest. In the forest tower are the trees of your passions—anger, pride, vanity, envy, avarice, fear, gluttony, lust, and sloth. Something strong is required to keep you going in such terrifying places.

Stillness

The energy necessary to keep going is still and unmoving rather than boisterous and reactive. The ego has an automatic reaction to pain, physical or psychological. You stop breathing for a moment, tense up the muscles, and prepare to either fight or flee. This is how type (the ego) takes over, trying to protect you from the experience. It believes it is all alone in the cage, except maybe for that tiger waiting to devour it! However, when the ego tenses up, the free flow of energy stops. The energy behind whatever painful emotion you are experiencing does not flow in, around, then out of the body. Instead it stops and becomes lodged in some organ or set of muscles. It gets "stuck" and eventually congeals into part of the system of your type's particular passion. In spiritual work, when your passion is awakened, you do better to simply go still. Take a deep breath, become the observer, and watch without acting on it. I am not sure that you can really "relax" when in the grip of your passion, but it *is* possible to be still. When something painful grabs your attention, take a deep breath . . . and remember to smile! Try to let the smile drop down from your mouth to your heart and from there to your belly. Pay attention to your body and its sensations rather than to your mind and its story. Get curious. You have just slipped down the stairwell into the magical cave. Smile! Like Zhou, you are in that transition from sleep to awake. You are now ready to enter the Pivot of Dao, the place from which you can begin the transformation of the ten thousand things.

This requires practice, however, and so the training for spiritual transformation begins with self-quieting. The first stage of self-quieting is some daily practice of meditation. It can be done sitting or moving, from a Christian, Buddhist, Daoist or whatever perspective. But it has to be done. You can't find the path through the dark forest if you are forever chattering, texting or twittering. Chapter 14 of the *Inward Training* (*Nei-yeh*), an early Daoist text on meditation asks what it means to be liberated by *Dao*. It states:

> The answer resides in the calmness of the mind
> When your mind is well ordered, your senses are well ordered.
> When your mind is calm, your senses are calmed.
> What makes them well ordered is the mind;
> What makes them calm is the mind.
> By means of the mind you store the mind:
> Within the mind there is yet another mind.
> That mind within the mind: it is an awareness that precedes words.

The text implies a sequence of steps. First, use the mind to order one's life and calm one's senses. Next use the mind to "store" the mind. It does not say "silence" the mind, but "store" the mind. This suggests a process of creating space for storage rather than gutting a structure with the intent to knock it down. And indeed, chapter 13 of the same text describes how the mind within the mind will come of its own accord:

> There is a numinous mind [*shen*] naturally residing within;
> One moment it goes, the next it comes,
> And no one is able to conceive of it.
> If you lose it you are inevitably disordered;
> If you attain it, you are inevitably well ordered.
> Diligently clean out its lodging place
> And its vital essence [*jing*] will naturally arrive.
> Still your attempts to imagine and conceive of it.
> Relax your efforts to reflect on and control it.

The suggestion is that the stillness one seeks, the "mind within the mind," cannot be attained once and for all, for it comes and goes. It "wants" to arrive, however, for that is its nature. Our only task is to keep its lodging place clean. It will show up all by itself. When it shows up, it will unite the spiritual energy [*shen*] of the upper *dan tian* with physical energy [*jing*] of the lower one. When both higher and lower *dan tian* act in consort, a person's emotional responses and even physical perceptions change. The energy begins to move freely in, around, and through the body. This is what will create the capacity to act effortlessly and without the use of force. And why does this unification take place all by itself? *Because it is already there albeit unrecognized.* Several lines later, at the beginning of chapter 14, the *Nei-yeh* continues:

The Way (*Dao*) fills the entire world,
it is everywhere that people are,
but people are unable to understand this.

How can the Way be everywhere and yet remain hidden? This is really the central problem of any meditation practice. How can what I am looking for be said to be "already within me" when I keep failing to find it day after day? The most common answer people give is, "There is something wrong with me; I am not doing it right." The next most common one is, "The whole thing is a hoax; there is nothing to be found." The Daoist sage would reply: "Both answers are right—and both wrong." Daoism's basic credo is that *Dao* cannot be found existing by itself. It is always hidden within the particular, so when you seek the Absolute all by itself, you are looking in the wrong place. There is no such thing. And when you complain that there is nothing to be found, you are in one sense quite correct. There is no-thing to be found, for all that really exists is the inseparable continuity of *Dao* to *de*. The freedom promised by Way-making, or the practice of *Dao*, is the realization that you can find the universal presence (*Dao*) only when you directly apprehend one particular (*de*) because they are inseparable.

From the Daoist point of view, the bottom line is that there is only one reality comprised of *Dao* and *de* together. There is no Presence *outside of and independent from* the ten thousand things. In other words, there was no time in which *Dao* carried on prior to the begetting of *de*. *Dao* and *de* implicate one another and always have. In your practice of the Enneagram, there is no "tenth type" you should be striving for. Nor can you find a state of mind that forever does away with your type. There is only you, always and forever self-so-ing as you were meant to do. Similarly, there is no separate and independently existing "I" to search for in your meditations. Remember the *Nei-yeh's* advice about the numinous mind: "Still your attempts to imagine and conceive of it. Relax your efforts to reflect on and control it." You cannot ever catch hold of it, even though it is always present, even in your failure to locate it. From a Daoist perspective, there is no Supreme Being or God or Buddha-nature to be grasped as a separate graspable entity; there is only unspeakable infinite goodness hiding within every event. Presence *is* but remains truly hidden within the world. The process of discovering it is what *Zhuangzi*, in a monumental understatement, called "looking for the obvious.

Presence

I began this book with the suggestion that the human infant arrives in Presence. Before subjective self has been clearly divided from objective other, Presence is experienced as shared awareness, or the intuition that all awareness is the same. It just happens that due to the way the human mind develops, single-pointed awareness gradually begins to experience reality through a prism that breaks reality into two parts—subject and object. Your adult spiritual task is to put this prism back together, to begin seeing with eyes that not only perceive the object but your own act of seeing at the same time. Awareness of your own seeing is the doorway into a type of consciousness that is pure presence. When you reach that, you realize that you cannot be alone.

This is the third and probably most important central principle of spiritual work: you are not alone. You are not alone because you participate in the one-pointed singularity of awareness, Presence itself. This Presence is not an abstraction. It is not a mechanical energy or force. It is mindful and loving. I myself do not think of it is a "person," for to me the notion of personhood suggests something like us, an individual that has a point of view and a certain way it wants the universe and all the beings in it to evolve. I do not think Presence is a person in this all-too-human sense. Nonetheless, it is intelligent and above all loving. Not loving in the selfish sense of "wanting to make you mine" but loving in the larger sense of wanting each being to "self-so." I believe that if you want to grow spiritually deeper, you must seek an encounter with the loving nature of this Presence. You must call upon it. There are many forms of prayer. Many of them are actually quite selfish. But there is one form every spiritual seeker, without exception, must learn. However worded, it is always the same:

> As yet I am not skilled in heavy grief,
> so this colossal dark weighs down on me.
> But *Thou* art: brace thyself, breach my cave.
> Lay the full weight of thy hand on me,
> and I the buried depths of my soul on thee.

Finally, even though infants may not be able to understand these lines of Rilke, they still have much to teach us about the spiritual life. They teach us that it is possible to be present, to be joyful and to share in one awareness. They teach us that we are naturally born to seek one another. The only permanently debilitating trauma a child can suffer is to be alone. Not alone as in a room all by yourself, but alone as is no one sees, understands, or cares about what you experience. My years of working with children have taught me that they can come through almost any traumatic incident without great lasting damage—so long as they do not go through it all alone. The same holds true for each of us as we walk through the dark forest. You must find your own unique path, but you do not walk it alone. It does not matter how you conceive this Presence. Call it the Higher Power or the Christ; call it Holy Spirit, Buddha, or *Dao*. It is of no importance *what* you call it. It is utterly important however that you *address* it, and faithfully wait for it to appear.

Eternal Process

The fourth and last central principle is, as the *Nei-yeh* warns, that our human awareness of Presence will continue to appear and disappear. One of the great joys of spiritual work is that the path through the forest is not always dark. The more deeply one walks into it, the more frequently it seems an enchanted place. And then, sometimes quite suddenly, the moonlit glade dappled by fireflies disappears and one encounters a briar patch infested by ghoulish insects. Quite naturally one wants to cut short the marches through tangles inhabited by demons and to hang out in meadows lit by glow-worms. But in this world, one cannot remain anywhere forever, for it is the nature of light to create shadows, and it is the nature of darkness to birth the dawn. *Dao* is said to be changeless, but it is forever moving. Ancient Daoists knew this and developed a spiritual methodology that emphasized process and change over states and stages. They placed the key to the transformation of things in "not choosing one thing rather than another." And that involves the heart. One can meditate forever. One can even reach the Void. But without the heart, even the Way becomes a seductive sterility. In order to fully appropriate it, one must encounter *Dao* as the cosmic Smile, a welcoming and loving presence hiding the world within the world. The spiritual life then begins to take on the character of a great game of hide and seek, and one can truly say with Tagore: "With the tune of thee and me all the air is vibrant, and all ages pass with the hiding and seeking of thee and me" (*Gitanjali*, No. 71).

The great, no, the magnificent paradox of human life is that we are living vessels of consciousness sailing inexorably through time and space toward physical death. We are fragments of the Formless Living One, yet we know we shall die. This fusion of eternal and time-limited does not easily co-exist. Nevertheless, we are meant to be this way. It is our destiny. It is not a mistake; it is not a condition waiting to be rectified. It is how the primal energy or absolute power or divine being or highest good takes form as *de*. Personal liberation, release, or enlightenment does not require that we leave the body behind and ascend to the absolute. Nor does it require that divinity obliterate or traverse a space of ontological separation between itself and us in order to "save" us. It only requires that we recognize and embrace our situation exactly as it is. And what is our situation? Listen one last time to the poet:

> On the seashore of endless worlds children meet. The infinite sky is motionless overhead and the restless water is boisterous. On the seashore of endless worlds the children meet with shouts and dances.
>
> They build their houses with sand and they play with empty shells. With withered leaves they weave their boats and smilingly float them on the vast deep. Children have their play on the seashore of worlds.
>
> They know not how to swim, they know not how to cast nets. Pearl fishers dive for pearls, merchants sail in their ships, while children gather pebbles and scatter them again. They seek not for hidden treasures, they know not how to cast nets.
>
> The sea surges up with laughter and pale gleams the smile of the sea beach. Death-dealing waves sing meaningless ballads to the children, even like a mother while rocking her baby's cradle. The sea plays with children, and pale gleams the smile of the sea beach.
>
> On the seashore of endless worlds children meet. Tempest roams in the pathless sky, ships get wrecked in the trackless water, death is abroad and children play. On the seashore of endless worlds is the great meeting of children.

Rabindranath Tagore, *Gitanjali,* No 60.

The poem is one of such great compassion. It perceives the incongruity of our situation with utter clarity, yet it does so with complete acceptance and love. It tells us that we live between an infinite motionless consciousness and a restless, boisterous ocean of physicality. On that shore, our adult egos build kingdoms and societies, start companies, go bankrupt, attend seminars, and write books. They set out on adventures and journeys, trying to live like heroes on the vast deep even though they are sailing in boats made of leaves looking for castles made of sand. They dive for treasure and cast endless, endless tangles of nets. But our souls, like children, care not for swimming or finding treasure. They are more interested in the pebbles right in front of our noses. They do not fear the powerful forces that surround us, rock us to and fro, and at times devastate us. The sea plays with us, and the sea beach, this tiny isle on which we play, can only smile palely. On this endless shore of presence, beneath the infinite sky and the trackless sea, we have met. In the face of certain death, we greet one another with shouts and dances. Presence is our great meeting place. Presence is the mother who rocks us with such compassion.

You can be free this very moment. Smile! You are already here, exactly as you are, dancing in the arms of the endlessly moving *Dao*, the Field of Presence.

Appendix A: Beginning and/or Deepening a Meditation Practice

The Inner Smile

The central practice of Daoism is called the Inner Smile. The Inner Smile can be used with any meditation practice: Christian, Buddhist, Sufi, or Daoist. You simply place the tip of the tongue against the palate behind the front upper teeth. Then gently smile, not so much with your lips but inwardly. The smile actualizes your intention not just to be mindful of what arises within awareness but to welcome it. Feel what happens inside your mouth when you try this. The space softens and feels slightly more expansive. Next gently let the softness drop down to the heart. Now you are adding the energy of the heart to your energy of paying attention. You should now feel an even more powerful softening of your experience. Finally, allow the softness to extend all the way down to the belly. Try this whenever you meditate. Try it on and off throughout the day. It can be done in 15 to 20 seconds. It is especially helpful when one of your ugly toads shows up.[15]

---

15 For a complete description of the Inner Smile, its origin, meaning, and ways to deepen one's practice of it, see Michael Winn's *Way of the Inner Smile: Self-Acceptance—Tao Path to Inner Peace.* It is available free on line at www.HealingDao.com.

Beginning a Meditation Practice

One day it will become clear to you that a daily spiritual practice is an absolute necessity. That may seem strange given all I have been saying about how "doing" and putting out effort cannot bring about inner peace. What is a daily practice if it is not *doing* something?

Actually, the whole purpose of a daily practice is to stop doing. Meditation, yoga, *qigong,* and centering prayer all have one basic goal: the cessation of your effort. They are techniques, indeed, and therefore one needs to practice them in order to become skillful. But the skill in question is the ability to let go and *stop* doing. Many readers of this book will already have a daily practice. Some of you have attempted one in the past, perhaps repeatedly, but for one reason or another have given it up. If this is the case, don't despair. That's the way most of us get started. For years I tried to meditate, and for years I found it impossible to stay faithful to any daily regimen. The change that allowed me to shift from making attempts to making sure is not easy to describe. The most important change is that today I do not *try* to meditate—I just love to stop doing all the other stuff. It is not that my meditations are always deep, serene, still, and all those luscious things. They are not. But I love that hour each morning when I get to do nothing except witness the river of life flowing through me. I love that period in the afternoon when a *qigong* form takes me into movement that seems so still. These are my times. They are just for me, and I love what they bring me over time. If you are considering beginning a practice, I urge you to make your goal learning to *love* your practice rather than learning to *do* it.

As you begin (or begin again), there are some practical considerations. They mostly fall into the categories of where, when, and what. One can meditate anywhere (I include yoga, centering prayer, *qigong,* or any other form of practice, as well) but a successful practice requires a choice of place. It should be a place of privacy and quiet, removed from the TV, telephone, and noise of others in the house. Request to not be disturbed except for emergencies. Make it a pleasant place with the kind of lighting and decor that puts your mind at ease. If you use a chair, select one that allows you to sit comfortably but erect. You want both feet to rest on the floor or at least on a cushion, and you want your spine to be straight so that you can feel an open column from your tailbone to the top of your skull. If you sit Indian style you probably want a proper cushion. It may take you a while to find best the place for you and to outfit it the way that works best. Put some thought into it. The place you are making is a sacred one.

Another important choice is when to meditate. It will be different for everyone. The only rule I can offer you with any certainty is this: choose a definite time of day, and do not vary from it unless absolutely necessary. A random schedule of meditation will invariably be a short-lived one. You will probably never be able to come up with a time of day when you are not tired. The best you can do is to make sure your daily schedule gives you sufficient sleep, and begin your meditation period with some exercises that awaken your body without breaking a sweat or making you breathe hard. (Use a brush or simply your own hands to rub your face, arms, body, and legs. It gets the *Qi* flowing!) Then stay with the schedule long enough to allow your metabolism to become accustomed to it. You may initially find yourself sleepy, especially as you begin your meditation period, but after several months, you probably will discover that you no longer start each period by nodding off or even falling asleep. (If you do fall asleep, let it be! Thank the life energy for giving you a rest and come back again the following day.)

How long to meditate is a sub-question of when to meditate. If you are just beginning, five minutes is sufficient. Within a year or so you, would like to increase that to a half hour. Ultimately, you want at least one hour per day, either all at once or broken into two halves. It is useful to have a timer so you won't be tempted to keep eyeing the clock. Try to find one that has a pleasant rather than an annoying ring.

The biggest and hardest question is what form of practice to choose. There are literally thousands of choices. I beg you not to try them all! Whatever you choose, stay with it for at least three months before trying something else. Meditative practices basically divide into two broad categories: sitting and moving. Most forms of centering prayer and Buddhist meditation are done while seated. Yoga, *qigong,* and ecstatic dancing involve physical movement. I find a combination of both works best for me. For years I tried only sitting meditations. During that period I never came to love to meditate. Everything changed for me when I was introduced to *qigong*, which is simultaneously a moving meditation and a meditation on movement. I think that the reason for this is that I am a mental type, and in my mental way, I was sitting in meditation trying *not* to think. Of course, it was not working. When I began *qigong,* I acquired a new focus—my body and the energies moving through it. The more that became my focus, the quieter my mind became. I am not promising that taking up *qigong* will do the same for you, of course. I am saying that it is imperative you find some way to allow your head, heart, and body to work together as you meditate.

The simplest way to begin is by following the breath. Breathing is the basic exchange between you and the life force. The inner lining of your lungs is the skin that touches its energy most directly. When I say follow the breath, I am talking about two things. The first is literal—observe the inhaling and exhaling of air. The second is metaphorical and more important—observe the flow of *Qi* in and out of your body. This sounds a bit strange at first. What flow, of precisely what energy? What I mean here is that you have two bodies, not one. Your physical body breathes by taking air through the nostrils or mouth down into the lungs and exhaling it back out. But as you do this, you can also imagine taking your breath into your belly, below the solar plexus muscle, where your lungs do not extend. Now you are observing what is called your energy body. Go ahead and try it. As you inhale, imagine the breath going to the lower *dan tian* about two fingers below your navel and about two fingers' deep behind the skin. Smile!

If you are beginning a practice, this is all you need do. Your goal is simple. You are trying to find that place in your belly. By "trying to find," I mean you are learning to experience that location. It is one you probably never paid much attention to before, and you don't know how to bring it into awareness. It is called the third or lower *dan tian* by the Chinese. The Japanese call it *hara*. The Sufis call it the *kath*. If they all found it, you can, too.

As you begin to locate it, watch what happens to your body. Many people feel an opening up or sense of expansiveness. It may feel very relaxed yet firm and grounded at the same time. Whatever happens, your only purpose is to observe. While you do that you will undoubtedly find yourself thinking, imagining, planning, feeling emotion, or making judgments. These are nothing but programs running on the hard drive of your ego. You need not try to stop them. In fact, the more you try, the more resistant they will become. You just gently label them: "thinking," "feeling," "planning," etc. And go back to watching the breath entering and leaving the lower *dan tian*. Your job is not to stop the mind from operating; it is only to observe what arises while keeping one's focus on the breath. And keep smiling!

Some people find that a short mantra helps them stay focused. (In my experience, this is particularly helpful for heart types since it moves them slightly toward the upper *dan tian.*) If you want, you can use one for the entire meditation. Or you can use one for only four or five minutes, then move to different one. Stringing three or four together will make a nice fifteen minute cycle.

Some teachers suggest that the student try to count each breath cycle. You keep counting until you reach twenty-one cycles, and then you begin at one again. Any time you notice that your attention has been drifting you go back to one. At first, you may find you cannot get to five without being distracted. However, your capacity to remain focused will gradually increase. Within a few months, you will find you can do it for ten or twenty breaths. As the years go by you can reach well into the hundreds. (Caution: for those readers are competitive by nature, counting breaths can turn into a "beat my last record" effort and for that reason is best left alone.) By the time you have learned to do this, your mind will have greatly quieted, and your attention span will have greatly increased. You are training yourself to stay focused and quiet so that you can be *receptive*. That is the whole point of a meditation practice. It is simply a technique that teaches you to stop *doing* so that you can allow the "mind within the mind" to arrive instead.

Your practice will be far more likely to prosper if you do it in some way that connects you to others. You do not always have to be in a group, but meditation is more powerful when done with others. Having a teacher or mentor is a tremendous help.

What will happen if you continue with your practice? What will happen is *you*—your process, your unique unfolding, and your continued self-discovery. Your path is a path no one else has ever taken nor ever will.

Each of your breaths is a new, never before taken exchange of energy with the universe. Meditating on the breath is a powerful method of becoming ever more aware of the singular and unique relationship you have with all of Being. Take a moment to ponder the following poetic description of how meditation gradually "becomes" the one who meditates. It opens Part 2 of Rilke's *Sonnets to Orpheus*. The original German repeatedly rings with the sound "*ein,*" a word stem which connotes singularity, onceness, and presence. Notice the first word. It is the German verb meaning "to breathe", and is a literal borrowing from the Sanskrit *atmen*, itself a derivative of Atman, the universal breath of life in Hindu spirituality.

> Breathing, you invisible poetry!
> Constant in-and-around-each-being
> exchange of pure worldspace; counterpoint,
> in which I rhythmically occur.
>
> Singular wave, whose
> gradual ocean I become;
> you the most spare of all possible seas,—
> space gatherer.
>
> How many of these spaces have already
> entered me. So many zephyrs,
> become like my own child.
>
> Do you recognize me, breath, you, now complete within my chambers?
> You, at once the glossy bark,
> rounded limb and leaf of all my words.

R.M. Rilke, *Sonette an Orpheus,* Sonett I Part II, translated by W. Schafer. The original German text is as follows:

> *Atmen, du unsichtbares Gedicht!*
> *Immerfort um das eigne*
> *Sein rein eingetauschter Weltraum. Gegengewicht,*
> *in dem ich mich rhythmisch ereigne.*
>
> *Einzige Welle, deren*
> *almähliches Meer ich bin;*
> *sparsamstes du von allen möglichen Meeren,—*
> *Raumgewinn.*

Wie viele von diesen Stellen der Räume waren schon
innen in mir. Manche Winde
sind wie mein Sohn.

Erkennst du mich, Luft, du, voll noch einst meiniger Orte?
Du, einmal glatte Rinde,
Rundung und Blatt meiner Worte.

Simple *Qi* Breathing

If you just began to meditate within the past month or so, please skip what follows for now. Best to stay with one practice until you have some mastery over it before beginning something new. However, if you already have some facility with sitting meditation, this practice may interest you. It is really nothing more than an adaptation of a basic *qigong* practice to a sitting meditation.

You may do this meditation either standing, lying down on your back, or seated, although I personally find it works best if I stand for a while before sitting down. As always, begin by getting the *Qi* to flow. Gently shake and rub your hands, face, chest, and legs—just enough to feel some tingling but not so much as to break a sweat or grow short of breath. Stand with your knees relaxed, your feet about shoulder width from one another. Smile! Place your hands on your belly, fingers gently spread. You will find your thumbs and forefingers making a kind of natural circle around the navel. Begin your normal practice of following the breath to the lower *dan tian*. You will feel the belly expand with each inhale and get smaller with each exhale. You will find that as you inhale you naturally want to shift your weight ever so slightly onto your toes and that your pelvis lifts forward and up just a tad while your chin tends to rise slightly. As you exhale the opposite tends to happen. Your weight shifts slightly to your heels, your pelvis relaxes down and back, and your whole body sinks slightly. Quite naturally, your whole body is beginning to make a small circular motion with each breath—forward and up upon inhaling, backward and down upon exhaling. Take some time to get a sense of this circular movement. It is important because it expands the straight up and down perception of breathing into a three dimensional sphere.

Once this becomes familiar, place your attention upon the exhalations. Feel the front of your belly contract toward the spine. With some firmness, but without force, feel the belly space close until you imagine it to be about the size of a pearl. Pause for as long as feels natural given your rhythm of breathing, then feel the pearl expand as you inhale once more. Continue this until you are so familiar with the process that it becomes routine. And keep smiling!

Now imagine that all of your skin is one giant lung. With each breath, you expand like a balloon and then contract again. The body you are imagining here is not your physical body; it is your energy body. It is roughly the same size you are but somewhat larger, and its contours are rounded and flexible. To make this more concrete, let your hands come free from your belly until they are a few inches away from your skin. Your hands now symbolize the boundaries of your energy body. Let them gently move away as you inhale and back towards the belly with each exhale. Let yourself become familiar with the expansion of the energy body to a size larger than your physical body and then back down to the pearl located within your lower *dan tian*.

If you wish, you can use this technique to work on the Pivot of Dao for your Enneatype. For example, if you are a One, your virtue is Serenity, and your vice or passion is Anger. Breathe in serenity; breathe out anger. The Pivot of Dao for you is the place where they merge and transform into one another. You may continue to stand until the end of your meditation, or if you prefer, you can take your seat and complete the meditation in a seated position. Be careful to maintain awareness of the cycle of up and forward, down and backward while you are seated. Remember, keep smiling! Continue this practice until it becomes second nature. You don't want to need to think about it. It works best if you let it all happen by itself.

Counterforce *Qi* Breathing

The following is an adaptation of a more advanced *qigong* practice known as counterforce breathing. Do not begin this practice until simple *Qi* breathing has become automatic. It adds several complications, and although the new practice can be very powerful, the complications increase the possibility of turning the whole thing into a mental game.

If at any time you suspect that is happening to you, go back until the previous step is so automatic you no longer have to think about it.

Again, you can do this meditation either standing, lying down, or while seated, although for the purpose of introducing the meditation, I will assume you are standing. As always, begin the meditation by making the *Qi* flow—some gentle rubbing of hands together and of hands over arms, body, and legs will suffice. Then stand quietly to let the breath slow. Feel your body being pulled toward the earth. Feel your feet on the floor, or if sitting, your buttocks on the chair; let your shoulders fall slightly, even feel your cheeks being pulled gently down. Allow yourself to experience the earth's embrace.

Step One

Now begin simple *Qi* breathing with your hands on your belly. Remember, begin with the Inner Smile. Allow your breathing to find its own pace; let its rhythm settle in. When you feel comfortably settled, move your hands a few inches away from your belly, palms still pointing toward the center of the lower *dan tian*. However, contrary to what you were doing before, now move your hands *in* as you inhale and *away* as you exhale. Your hands are now following the movement of your breath, not your body. That is, they make a larger circle as you breathe out and a smaller one as you breathe in. Your belly is doing exactly the opposite. It contracts as you breathe out and expands as you breathe in. Allow that contrast to become familiar. Practice this stage of the meditation for a week or so before going on to the next stage.

Step Two

As your hands move gently inward with each inhale, notice the slight increase of energy in your palms. As your hands move away again with each exhale, notice the energy increase on the back of the hands. As you move them toward the body, the palms heat up ever so slightly. As you move them away from the body, the backs of your hands tingle a little. Once you can feel this energy moving, turn your attention to your arms. See if you can feel the same thing happening there. The inside of the arms sense a movement of energy at each inhale, the outsides at each exhale. Follow the flow even further if you can. Upon inhaling, you can sense the energy moving from the palms to the inner arms all the way to the chest and tummy. Upon exhaling, you can sense it flowing along the back of the hands to the outside of the arms and around the shoulders and back. As you try to find these energetic currents in your body, it may help to vary the amount of movement your hands make with each breath. Less movement, or perhaps a little more movement—which amount helps you sense the flow of energy better?

Stay with this stage until it, too, becomes familiar and simple. When it does, you will notice that your energy body now seems concentrated in a kind of sphere. It contracts inside the circle formed by your palms, inner arms, chest, and tummy every time you breathe in; it expands outward from your knuckles, arms, shoulders, and back each time you breathe out. As before, continue this practice until it becomes second nature. You don't want to need to think about it. It works best if you let it all happen by itself.

Step Three

Continue to feel the movement of your energy body's circle inward to center with each inhale and radiating outward with each exhale. Gradually shift the center of this sphere until it rests inside the lower *dan tian*. You will now notice that when you breathe in, the ball of energy collapses toward the "pearl" between your navel and spine. When you breathe out, it expands outward perhaps a few feet from your physical body. Let that become routine and semi-automatic.

Now let yourself become aware (if you have not already naturally done so) that the movement of this sphere is directly opposite to the movement of your physical belly. When you breathe in, the belly or physical body expands while the energy body is contracting. When you breathe out, the physical belly is shrinking as the energy body expands. You are now aware of the counterforce movement. Your body physically reaches out as the life energy enters; your body contracts as it releases that energy back out to the *Qi* field. The *Qi* field in turn is doing the opposite. As you breathe in, the field is exhaling and entering you; as you breathe out, the field is inhaling the energy you give back to it. The two of you are engaged in yet another type of counterpoint—a slow, methodical, and wonderfully tender form of love-making.

You can now use this technique to work on the Pivot of Dao for your Enneatype in an even more powerful way. Imagine two spheres. One is expanding as the other contracts. When the second begins to expand, the first starts to contract. Let one sphere be your virtue. Let the other represent your vice. Then watch them interpenetrate, moving in and out right through one another. In a short time, you will probably lose track of which is virtue and which is vice. For example, if you are a One, you will no longer simply be breathing in Serenity and breathing out Anger as you were during simple Qi breathing. You will instead be transforming the egoic cycle of trying to control anger by becoming compliant to standards into a balanced cycle of allowing *yang* expansiveness to mingle with *yin* receptivity in a clear (serene) awareness of the self-so as-it-is-ness of whatever arises in consciousness. At the center of this cycling energy will be you, neither angry nor trying to improve, but just as you are. Smile!

Stay with this stage of the practice long enough for it to become second nature. If at any point you find yourself needing to think about what you are doing, go back to a simpler previous stage.

Step Four

When you have become adept at Counterforce breathing, you may want to add this last step to your practice. It is called Stillpoint Breathing.

Find the spot of stillness at the center of the two spheres that are moving in counterpoint. There is a place where nothing moves, around which everything else is moving. Draw your attention to this place, and at the end of each exhale, say "stop" very gently. Hear the mini-second of stillness following the period after the word "stop." Stop all thought, stop all effort, and stop all attempts to pay attention to the movements or the energy patterns or anything else. You have reached your core, the motionless center of all movement, your Pivot of Dao. Gradually, you will find yourself accessing this place of stillness more quickly and more often and remaining within it longer.

I find this a very powerful meditative practice, but it takes time to learn. Don't rush through the learning period. If you do, it will only be a complicated mental game distracting you from your ultimate purpose.

Appendix B: History and Philosophy of the Enneagram

A Brief History of the Enneagram

As we said at the beginning, the Enneagram is a diagram, a "nine-writing" that purports to describe a fundamental law of how change happens. As you know from Figure 1, the diagram is generally drawn as a circle in which are inscribed an equilateral triangle and an irregular hexagon. The symbol's origins go back some six thousand years to Sumer (present day Iraq and Iran). No one knows how the Enneagram might have been used in those early millennia. The symbol is found in rocks and bricks from that era, but nothing is known of its associated teaching, which was likely linked in some way to Zoroastrianism. We know very little about its development in the orient until the ninth century of the present era, when the great Persian mathematician Al-Khwarizmi borrowed Hindu numerals and the concept of zero from India. Once true zero was introduced, basic arithmetic computations encountered certain disturbances. (In Christian Europe, zero was considered such a satanic force that it was not allowed until the sixteenth century.) One of them is the infinitely repeating decimal. For example, when unity is divided by nine, the answer is a number which cannot be completely written, e.g., 0.11111 *ad infinitum*. Something similar happens when unity is divided by either three (0.33333 . . .) or six (0.166666 . . .). Lastly, dividing unity by seven yields another repeating decimal which contains all the remaining integers in the order of 0.142857142857142

. . . and so on indefinitely. The Enneagram may have been used as a simple way of communicating these intriguing results. Its outer circle represented unity. The inner triangle represented the infinitely repeated results of dividing unity by nine, three, and six. The irregular hexagon, arranged around the numerals 1, 4, 2, 8, 5, and 7, represented the similarly infinite quotient yielded when unity is divided by seven. The whole thing seems to have been taken as a symbol of nature's mysterious process of endless self-creation.

The tradition that carried the Enneagram over the millennia to us is often called the "perennial philosophy," a term coined by Aldous Huxley in 1945. It was so named because it appears with similar features across cultures and ages. Although its roots go back to ancient Persia and India, the perennial philosophy had a heavy influence upon and was in turn shaped by the mystery religions of Greece and by Pythagoras, Plato, and the Gnostics. From there the tradition entered Europe. It fell into immediate disfavor during the earliest Christian period when expectations of Jesus' literal return to establish a political kingdom overrode the more mystical Gnostic version of his message. However, it experienced something of a renaissance during the third and fourth centuries, partly through a group known as the Desert Fathers. These were Christian monks, many of whom were followers of Origen, a Christian theologian heavily influenced by Gnosticism (and roundly condemned for this by several church councils). These men and women left what they perceived as the chaos and corruption of a decadent Roman empire for the simplicity and tranquility of the deserts of Egypt and the Middle East.

Spiritual training within the perennial philosophy emphasized still, non-judgmental observation of one's own internal mental and emotional states. Today we call this practice the cultivation of the Inner Observer. Over the centuries, descriptions of how different students reacted to the practice were categorized. Each type had its own signature emotion and its own signature manner of perceiving the world. The first known person to systematically list these reactions appears to be a fourth-century monk named Evagrius of Pontus, who listed eight types of monks: those whose hearts were troubled by anger, pride, vainglory, sadness, avarice, gluttony, lust, or sloth. (He seemed to have missed fear, the signature emotion of type Six.) Two hundred years later, Pope Gregory the Great codified seven of these emotional reactions or "passions" as the seven cardinal sins. They were called cardinal from the Latin *cardo* meaning hinge or pivot because they were considered "lynchpin" moral structures that impeded spiritual progress. Curiously, one of Evagrius' monks, he of the vainglorious heart, failed to make Gregory's list. We don't know why this one failed to make the cut. It may be that vanity is harder to discern than the other passions. It might also be that by the end of the sixth century, when the Christianity had become firmly established as the dominant political power of a Roman Empire struggling to reinvent itself, vanity was no longer regarded an undesirable moral quality by Gregory, a pope who would go down in history as "the Great."

The perennial philosophy experienced a second European renaissance toward the end of the first millennium. The major port of entry was Spain, which was invaded by the Moors in 714. For the next five hundred years, the Iberian Peninsula became the focal point of contact among Muslims, Christians, and Jews. Much of the contact was warlike, but for a brief time in the twelfth century, Spain flourished as the most enlightened kingdom of Europe. Its universities were the best on the continent. Christian, Jewish, and Muslim professors held equal status in a brief but remarkable florescence of tolerance and respect. Along with medicine and mathematics were taught the philosophies of ancient Greece and Mesopotamia. Included were the mystical traditions of Sufism, which had incorporated elements of the perennial philosophy into Islam.

Even the crusades sometimes turned into unintended sources of entry for the perennial philosophy. For example, it is said that at the beginning of the thirteenth century, a young Italian named Francesco Bernardone went to Damascus with the intention of converting the sultan to Christianity. There he supposedly encountered a teacher named Shams of Tabriz. Soon after the meeting, the young soldier returned to Italy. He experienced a series of visions that left him with the stigmata (the wounds of the crucified Christ mystically imprinted on his own body). We know that young officer today as Francis of Assisi, the gentle saint who wrote the marvelous Canticle to the Sun.[16] The Arabic word for sun is *shams*, and the Canticle may also be read as Francis' homage to his teacher. The same Shams had another student, a non-European. We know that other student today as the great Sufi mystic and poet Rumi.

Since the Middle Ages, the oral tradition of Enneagram teachings regarding nine personality types and how they react as they begin the practice of developing the inner observer was kept alive mainly within various Sufi communities of the Middle East. It was reintroduced into Europe in the early twentieth century by George Gurdjiev who had learned it as a young man in present day Afghanistan. In the 1970s, the system was introduced to the United States by a Chilean psychiatrist-psychologist named Claudio Naranjo. Naranjo had come to the United States in the 1960s on a Fulbright scholarship to work on the early computerized studies of personality dimensions, first with Gordon Allport at Harvard, and subsequently with Raymond Cattell at Illinois. He later moved to Berkeley and began work with Frank Barron. Around 1970, he returned to the dry deserts of northern Chile to study the Enneagram with a psychologist and Sufi master by the name of Oscar Ichazo. Naranjo later claimed that his study with Ichazo was the most important turning point of his career. He returned to Berkeley the following year, and in subsequent years gave continuing seminars on the subject. Among the early participants were A. H. Almaas, Sandra Maitri, Robert Ochs, Charles Tart, and Helen Palmer.[17] Palmer was the first American psychologist to publish descriptions of the Enneagram in the public domain, something that had previously been previously forbidden by its inner circle of teachers. Today one

16 I have read the preceding story about Francis of Assisi (in Ladinsky, 2002), but have never been able to verify it independently. As Chesterton once remarked about St. Francis, it is not important whether he really did all the things attributed to him; it's that he was the kind of man about whom they would tell such stories. The same is probably true of Shams.

17 Almaas, a pen name that is Arabic for "diamond," is the founder of the Diamond Heart school of spiritual growth. Maitri is an early associate of Almaas; Robert Ochs was a Jesuit priest; Tart is a founder of trans-personal psychology; and Palmer is a leading author and teacher of the Enneagram in the Narrative Tradition.

can find hundreds of books about the Enneagram, some very fine and some just awful. Readers who are new to the system may want to begin with a short but excellent book by David Daniels, M.D. called, *The Essential Enneagram* (2009), which will help you determine your own type. Helen Palmer's now classic work *The Enneagram: Understanding Yourself and the Others in Your Life* (1991) is then the next book to read. It has been translated into over twenty languages and is used all around the world to give students a fuller appreciation of the depth and wisdom of the Enneagram. A short annotated bibliography of books on the Enneagram can be found in Appendix C.

Philosophical Assumptions

The Enneagram's origins reach back through Sufism to ancient Persia. Like all of the perennial philosophy, it is based upon a fundamentally different metaphysics from that of empiricism, which is the dominant philosophy of modern Europe and North America. Empiricism begins with by assuming that "true" knowledge comes only from empirical observation and measurement. As a result of such an assumption, the only true reality can be the material world. The mind is regarded as an epiphenomenon of the chemical and electronic circuitry of the material brain. Its most highly developed products are logic and analysis, which can in turn be used to predict and control the material world.

The perennial philosophy is a little less optimistic than empiricism is about the powers of human logic and analysis. One might even say it is downright pessimistic. In fact, the perennial philosophy directly attributes the human spirit's sense of alienation from the natural world to the overuse of analysis and reason. In philosophical terms, the perennial philosophy is "non-dual." It assumes that there is only one reality, which is simultaneously material and spiritual, temporal and eternal, individual and universal. (More precisely, it says that what appear to our human eyes as the two separate orders of material and spiritual, temporal and eternal, individual and universal, are "not two".) Our day to day unenlightened mind separates these perceived dualities into opposing categories, which is why we feel fundamentally alienated from our original ground. In the perennial philosophy, the spiritual task of the individual person is almost always described as some form of "remembrance," some form of return to a prior state before the sense of separation arose.

From this you can see how the Enneagram will be terribly misunderstood if one thinks of it as nine compartments into which to file human personality types. To see it thus is to see it only through empiricist eyes. More fundamentally, the Enneagram of the perennial philosophy is a mapping of energetic blockages that prevent us from recognizing our actual unity with a universal Reality that fully and completely inhabits and pervades us at every moment.

I have made Daoism a major thread of this book because I believe that Daoism is an elegantly articulated version of the perennial philosophy that beautifully complements the traditional teachings of the Enneagram. Daoism arose as a reaction to Confucius, who lived approximately around the time of the Buddha. Confucius had offered an elegant, rigorous, and highly moral philosophy of life to ancient China. Its distinguishing features were the cultivation of piety, deference, and fidelity to ritual and tradition. In many ways it was the most ideal philosophy of life yet proposed in all of Asia. But Confucius happened to propose it just as feudal China began to assemble itself into an empire. It accomplished this, of course, in the usual way—through stubborn, prolonged, and brutal warfare. Within a century or so of Confucius' death, China found itself the intellectual repository of the loftiest moral philosophy yet known to mankind, the translation of which could nowhere be found in the concrete hardships and cruelties of its day-to-day existence. In this disillusioned milieu, Daoism arose as a reaction against the failed formalism of Confucianism.

Daoists took as their starting point the observation that the most common element of life is change itself. Wherever we look, we see cycles of growth and decay, leading to new growth, further decay, and yet more growth. Individual things come and go, but process is forever. In the Daoist view, there are no "things," there are only "becomings." The central insight that everything is process was articulated in a language that operated quite differently from our own. Classical Chinese, unlike Greek, Latin, and their modern offshoots, has no copula. That is, there is no verb "to be." You cannot say, "This is a chair." You can only say, "We call this chair." The language itself begs us to remember that conceptual knowledge is intimately linked to human choice. In the classical Chinese view of things, people don't "discover" reality; they co-create it. Such a creative choice necessarily involves emotion. The Chinese character *xin* is usually translated today as "mind." But the written character or ideograph for *xin* is actually an abbreviated sketch of the human aorta. Whoever designed that ideogram understood that a person knows through the heart as well as the head. A thing or an event appears the way it does as much because of our feeling about it as because of its formal characteristics. There is reciprocal causality between knower and known, and the "true" reality is the dynamic field that holds them together. Somewhat naturally then, the function of knowledge in Daoism is not to grasp the abstract essence of something in order to predict and dominate it; it is rather to align oneself with the event that is happening so as to achieve greater harmony with its natural flow.

The Daoists also understood something else that is central to any attempt to harness the energies of the Enneagram for personal spiritual growth. They observed that every movement carries within itself the beginnings of its own undoing. Strength is what is beginning to grow weak; darkness is what is about to turn into light. Birth is the commencement of dying; evil is the starting point of good. We westerners, dualists that we are, think of these qualities as contradictory. We place them at opposing ends of a straight line: strength vs. weakness, darkness vs. light, birth vs. death, evil vs. good. Daoists, however, see them as one energetic quality stretched out along the periphery of a wheel, whose different aspects implicate and give birth to one another. This is a fundamental paradigm shift that is of great practical importance for self-transformation.

I do not want to waste time debating which philosophical prism, empiricism or Daoism, is superior. In fact, I think that to even raise the question, "Which one is true?" is to fall back into the empiricist habit of looking for the "true" reality behind the appearances. All knowledge implies a point of view. My point of view is just my current myth about reality. True, we have some choice as to which myth we will use to understand the world. The only choice we cannot make is to have a no myth at all. In this regard, it is important to note that western classical empiricism was the first large scale intellectual tradition to claim that it had no myth. It presented itself as absolute knowledge, reality seen from no viewpoint at all, objective truth stripped of all subjective bias. That claim possessed only relative validity. The beauty of empirical science lies precisely in the fact that salt is sodium chloride in the fifth century as well as in the twenty-first, in New York as well as in Beijing, on the table of a pauper or of a king. Empirical science is the most brilliant strategy ever devised to investigate the physical environment's interrelationships. It only goes amuck when it alleges that the physical environment is the only one possible or worth investigating.

Let's take another look at that grain of salt. For western science, the "reality" or "true meaning" of anything is its essence, not its appearance or its feel. Essences are objective and unchanging. Their effects can be predicted. Appearances and feelings are notoriously subjective and changeable. They constantly take us by surprise. In the eyes of empirical science, salt is "really" a molecule composed of one atom of sodium and another of chlorine. The deliciously biting taste of salt on my tongue as I sip a margarita somewhere on the southwestern shore of Mexico is a happy but entirely subjective result of this molecular state of affairs, produced by electrochemical changes taking place somewhere between my tongue and my brain. And what about the plush golden sunset I enjoy while I sip my drink? Well, from a purely objective point of view, a sunset is merely the apparent movement of the sun caused by the rotation of the earth, while the vermillion sky is actually a specific frequency of visible light that happens to be more abundantly diffused when the sun is viewed through longer distances of atmosphere such as occur at sunset or sunrise. And what, finally, is the feeling of awe washing over me as I watch the sun slip into the Pacific Ocean? It is just a specific state of arousal/relaxation caused by electrochemical changes within my nervous system as the neurons of my optic nerve present the vermillion spectrum to the visual centers of my cortex (which, of course, has been pleasantly prepared for the experience by the alcohol in my margarita). I may enjoy the tastes and feelings far more than the explanations, but empiricist metaphysics nevertheless assures me that the explanations are more objectively "real" than my subjective experience.

Empiricism has influenced (some might say afflicted) European thought and culture for over five hundred years. The search for predictability within variety causes us to see the world as made up of things rather than events, for things seem more stable than processes. So our western eyes look at flowing water, but what they see is a river. Or they register the felt hopelessness and fear of a weathered face, but what they see is a street person. The search for predictability also leads us to value the abstract idea over the concrete experience. We want to know the temperature rather than to step outside and feel the air of this very day; we prefer digital to analog in just about every gadget; we think it more helpful to calculate the per capital income of Sudan than to ponder the photograph of a starving baby.

Empiricism has been spectacularly successful in making the physical world more understandable and more comfortable to live in. It put a man on the moon and brought him back again. It gave us electricity in our homes, gasoline in our SUVs, cell phones and I pods in our pockets. Yet parsing experience in this way also has led to what the twentieth century philosopher A. N. Whitehead called "misplaced concreteness." By this he meant that our modern world bestows greater reality to the abstract principle rather than to the flow of experience. We value the hidden substance more than the present manifestation. We cling to the changeless rather than to joyfully greet the creatively new. Ultimately, we fill our world with all kind of "objects," which in turn often seem to growl back to us their sullen, "I object!" Nonetheless, even if empiricist culture tends to make our everyday lives somewhat sterile and boring, most of us are happy to let it do so because every so often it also gives us the means to fly to Mexico in order to savor a sunset over a really good margarita.

The question is can we enjoy the useful fruits of empiricism without falling prey to its habit of draining experience until it becomes dreary and dry of feeling and imagination? Hopefully, we can. Otherwise, there will never again be any "real" reason to order margaritas as the sun slips into the Pacific off shore of Puerto Escondido.

Appendix C: Self-Transformation and the Pivot of Dao

I don't think anyone has ever suggested that there is a direct lineage between Daoism and the Enneagram, although both belong to a common world tradition of reflection upon mystical experience (the *philosophia perennis*). The question of how the two understandings relate or do not relate to one another is a long and complicated one. This book is meant to lay out a practical way to use the Enneagram for spiritual growth from a Daoist perspective. In the main text of the book, I tried not to distract the reader with philosophical or theoretical questions. However, some readers may want to examine the notion of the Pivot of Dao in a more precise and methodical way. Such an inquiry has its usefulness for understanding what transformation really means, that is, what actually happens for ordinary people like you and me as we use the Enneagram in our spiritual work.

We can approach the issue with the following question: "How many points of view are there in the Enneagram?" That is, does the Enneagram demonstrate that there are nine different points of view and only nine? Or is there a tenth, the "true" perspective? In other words, must we make do with just nine partial and limited ways to pay attention to, interpret, and react to life, or are we searching for the one true "essential" way to pay attention to, interpret, and react to it? The question is not an idle one; it goes to the heart of why we study the Enneagram. Are we trying to end up with a polished and more presentable Enneatype, or are we looking to create the "perfect person" who is beyond type? Or then again do we seek something else quite entirely?

Let us try to make this more concrete by considering two people in a hypothetical but not untypical situation. The first (possibly a Six) says, "Here am I, angry with you because you have stood in my way, preventing me from accomplishing what I wanted and needed to do, all the while posing as my friend. I am enraged as much by your hypocrisy as by your opposition." And the other (possibly a Nine) says, "Here am I, wounded by your unending and unfair criticism of me. I have never wished you ill and never tried to hurt you. But you make a monster of me to everyone, so much so I now avoid you at all costs." (Now in actuality most people would never be this direct with one another. They would probably say these things to friends and colleagues rather than to one another. Or perhaps they would simply repeat such thoughts to themselves in their heads.)

What is the true situation? Who is right, and who is wrong? Could both be right? Or both wrong? And how could we ever know? If there are nine and only nine points of view, it seems we are forever prevented from knowing the "total truth" about anything, for we can only see from our limited perspectives. On the other hand, there might be a tenth perspective, say that of "essence." The goal of spiritual work would then be to reach a deeper level of knowing that gives access to the capacity to understand events, people, and self as they actually are. If we reach it, we can transcend our type, get over our arguments, and find a way to live in true harmony within ourselves and with one another. The problem is: who could discover and teach that tenth view? Suppose I were the lucky one. Suppose I reached such a high level of spiritual awareness that I could now tell you in simple yet elegant language the true goal of life and how you can attain it. I become the enlightened guru and you the eager student. But I would still have to teach you about that goal and the manner of its attainment from my perspective as a Six, and you would still have to listen to me from your perspective of whatever type you happen to be. So the "spiritual truth," even if it exists, seems to be inherently unteachable. (Consider Jesus. He probably possessed the real deal, or was at least closer to it than anyone else, yet with all due respect to many good Christians, how much luck did he have transmitting the central core of his message to others?) So we are left with a dilemma. Either there are nine partial viewpoints, and we can never escape them, or there is a tenth true perspective but no one can show it to us in a way we are capable of grasping.

The same dilemma confronts us when we consider what is meant by the word "self." Who am I, really? Let's start with the obvious. (As we shall see later on, this is precisely *Zhuangzi's* advice on the matter.) I am at this moment here, sitting in front of this computer, writing these words. My "self" is "in" this body. Where? I am pretty sure it is not in my hair or my toenails, for I can cut them and nothing changes. I don't really want this to happen, but if my fingers or even my arms were to disappear, I would still have a self. If worse came to worst, they could even take my kidneys, lungs, or heart, and I could still have a sense of self. Only if they chopped off my head would my feeling of self cease to be, I think. So does that mean the self is in my head, my trunk, or somehow in their union? Let's place our bets on the head. Let's say the self is somehow bound up with the brain. No brain, no self. Now suppose I have a closed head injury. What parts of my brain can be damaged and rendered useless before self disappears? Suppose I could no longer walk, see, or speak. I would still have a sense of self. Suppose I had no memories and could not recall my name or where I live or grew up. Would I still have a self? It seems that the absence of memory would somehow make me less a self, for my identity would then seem somehow compromised. But would you be quite willing to say I had *no* self? And what if only brain stem activity were left after my accident? Suppose like Terri Schiavo, I lay in the hospital, breathing and regulating body temperature, but hardly anything more. Would I still be myself? Much less so, you say. But are you at last willing to say I would then be completely, totally not a self? People argue (sometimes bitterly) about that one.

The same problem arises when we look within. All we come upon is a ceaselessly changing landscape of thoughts, moods, imaginings, memories, and sensations. When we search for *who* is thinking, feeling, fantasizing, remembering, and sensing, however, we draw a blank. So are we nothing more than the products of our mind? Or is there an unseen reality underneath them that is our "true" self? This question is structured exactly the same way as the one we asked about whether there are nine or ten types. And as we were with that question, we are left with a seemingly unanswerable dilemma: either we are nothing but our categories of mind, or we are something so unseen and invisible that we can never quite catch hold of it. If we choose the first horn of the dilemma, our spiritual task becomes that of reconciling ourselves to the fate of being but an ephemeral shadow. If we elect the second, our duty is to meditate or pray until an inner spiritual spotlight finally illuminates everything from the viewpoint of the godhead. It seems to me that we have ample testimony from our own lives and from the lives of those around us that neither alternative works very well, at least not for normal people.

Finally, we encounter a similar dilemma regarding the Divine. Whether we call it God or Brahman or *Dao*, it eludes us in the same way that objective truth and self elude us. At times we may be convinced that this ultimate Source is the only ultimately real and significant Being, but we have to admit that it remains incomprehensible. At other times we achieve a compelling sense that it is present within each limited and partial being yet that awareness quickly seems to disappear from view. As with the first two questions about truth and self, we are left with the feeling that both options (there is but one Reality worth knowing and it is unknowable; the only reality we can know about is the commonplace one we usually perceive) are somehow right and somehow wrong.

The Pivot of Dao is an attempt to unravel these dilemmas. We spoke of it in previous chapters as we considered the point of transformation for each type. But we might apply it better if we understood it more deeply. As you already know, the metaphor for Pivot of Dao is taken from the hole at the center of a wheel into which the axle is mounted. The hole is empty. It is nothing but a space. Yet the space is exactly what is necessary for the wheel to function. Were the space not there, the wheel could not be used. The metaphor is first introduced in the second chapter of the *Zhuangzi*, one of the greatest Daoist texts, compiled more than twenty-three hundred years ago. It may be the densest philosophical text ever written. It certainly is not easy for the western reader.[18]

Chapter two of the *Zhuangzi* begins with a student observing his teacher, Ziqi of Nanquo, deep in meditation. Ziqi appears "in a trance, as though he had lost the counterpart of himself [his opposite]."[19] When the teacher awakes, the student asks, "What is this? You are no longer the man I saw yesterday." Ziqi replies, "This time I had lost my own self [my 'me']. You hear the pipes of men, don't you, but not yet the pipes of earth, the pipes of earth but not yet the pipes of Heaven?" The student isn't sure what Ziqi means by this business of the pipes, but he still wants to know what it means to lose one's "me," so he asks for the secret of it. The teacher's reply comes in the form of a parable:

> That hugest of clumps of soil [the earth] blows out a breath by name the "wind." Better if it were never to start up, for whenever it does ten thousand hollow places burst out howling, and don't tell me you have never heard how the hubbub swells! The recesses in mountain forests, the hollows that pit great trees a hundred spans round, are like nostrils, like mouths, like ears, like sockets, like bowls, like mortars, like pools, like puddles. Hooting, hissing, sniffing, sucking, mumbling, moaning, whistling, wailing, the winds ahead sing out AAAH!, the winds behind answer EEEH!, breezes strike up a tiny chorus, the whirlwind a mighty chorus. When the gale has passed, all the hollows empty, and don't tell me you have never seen how the quivering slows and settles!

The student doesn't realize for the moment that his teacher is describing the facts of meditation. He is really just struggling to keep up and so he plays for time: "The pipes of earth, these are the various hollows; the pipes of men, these are rows of tubes. Let me ask about the pipes of Heaven." The teacher doesn't bother to lecture his student about the pitfalls of literalism. He simply provides the student yet

18 In this regard, I am indebted to Brook Ziporyn's insightful commentary, "How Many Are the Ten Thousand Thing and I?" in Scott Cook's wonderful collection *Hiding the World in the World: Uneven Discourses on the Zhuangzi* (2003).

19 From time to time I have placed in brackets a more literal translation of the original Chinese than that used by the A. C. Graham translation of the *Zhuangzi*.

another clue to the original question about what it means to lose one's "me": "Blowing through the ten thousand differences so that each puts forth from itself; they all take their individualities from it— but who is the blower?"

The student still doesn't have a clue, so Ziqi decides to slow everything down a bit. A few lines further on, he spells out for his student what all the noises or the wind represent: "Pleasure in things and anger against them, sadness and joy, forethought and regret, change and immobility, idle influences that initiate our gestures—music coming out of emptiness, vapour condensing into mushrooms."

In other words, the piping of men represents the categories of the mind. Our thoughts, moods, memories, plans and sensations are noises produced by the wind. The real question remains *who* does the blowing? The teacher, as is typical in the *Zhuangzi*, does not provide an immediate answer, only a further clue: "Without an Other, there is no Self, without Self no choosing one thing rather than another."

Here the teacher is simply referring his student back to the original question of what does it mean to lose both one's opposite (Other) and one's me (Self). And that pointing back to the original question is the only answer he will give to the question of who blows the wind. *Zhuangzi's* final answer, given through the lips of Ziqi, is that *the self revealed in deep meditation is essentially a continuing question: Who am I?*

Why does he never give his student (and us) a direct answer to the question of who does the blowing? Because he knows that *any answer* will be false. The point of the question is that it cannot be answered in the ordinary conceptual way. The "who" is formless. It is Presence itself—still, spacious, eternal consciousness. To turn it into an object of thought is to miss it entirely, for it is pure subject.

Since *Zhuangzi* cannot give a direct answer in objective terms, he can only point to what he means. One of his favorite ways of "pointing" is to tell a story. In the last paragraphs of the chapter, he tells the story of Zhuang Zhou's butterfly dream, which you may recall from chapter 6. The "real" Zhuang Zhou is the one who upon awakening is unsure about whether he is the butterfly or Zhou the man. His true self is found in the act of positing a question (Who am I?) to which he gives no objective answer. This is Zhuangzi's final word on what is meant by losing one's "me."

In other words, to lose one's "me" is to stop taking a perspective and thus to refrain from positing an objective answer. When you affirm an objective answer, you have taken a particular perspective. This entails choosing one thing rather than another. Taking a particular perspective also implies a "self," which has posited an "other." The sage does not do this. Like Ziqi he knows that "without an Other, there is no Self, without Self no choosing one thing rather than another."

Why does taking a perspective, having an opinion, or saying that something is true or false imply choosing one thing rather than another? The Daoist would answer by observing that knowledge is not just an impartial analysis performed by the intellect; it is also a choice springing from the heart. As previously noted, the Chinese character *xin*, usually translated as "mind", should actually be translated as "heart-mind." Feelings always play a part in knowledge. Even scientifically derived concepts spring from a mind that has chosen a particular theoretical framework, a particular way of selecting the data, posing the question, and setting up the analysis. In everyday human interaction, the situation is even more driven by the heart. In daily life, we are usually far more deeply involved in "choosing one thing rather than another."

In the middle of the chapter, *Zhuangzi* moves ever more deeply into the reason why Dao is obscured (that is, why it is not better observed by humans). He begins a particularly dense section by saying that the Way is flawed due to "the lighting up of 'That's it; that's not it'." "That's it" is the way modern translators render the Chinese ideograph that signifies the act of affirming. The ideograph is read *shih*. *Shih* is an affirmation, but the affirmation is not just of fact. *Shih* means, "That's it" the way you might say it to a child who has just gotten the hang of riding his bike without training wheels: "That's it!". *Fei* means, "That's not it!" but with opposite emphasis. Ordinary people are said to *shih-fei* constantly, always of course from their personal point of view. (Think of our Nine and Six arguing about what made them so upset with each other.)

This brings us finally to the Pivot of Dao. *Zhuangzi's* language grows ever denser as he strives to shake us out of our ordinary modes of thinking:

> This is also that, that is also this. This has its own this/that [shih-fei] and that also has its own this/that [shih-fei]. So is there really a this/that or isn't there? When this and that no longer find anything to be their opposites, this is called the Pivot of Dao. Once the Pivot finds the center, so that it can respond infinitely without obstruction, this/self/right is unobstructed and inexhaustible, and that/other/wrong is equally unobstructed and inexhaustible. This is why I said there's nothing better than using the obvious.

The text is so thick we have to pry it apart piece by piece. The light of *Dao* is obscured when we "choose one thing rather than another." The first party to any argument (a "this") has his unique *shih-fei*, his own perspective, whereas the other (the "that") takes another usually opposite *shih-fei* as his own. In the example we have been using, each party has taken a stand in self, making the second party other. The Six is stuck in, "You thwarted me" while the Nine is stuck in, "You demonized me." Each asserts he speaks the truth and the other falsehood. Thus *Dao* is obscured. The only place from which awareness of *Dao* can be restored is the Pivot of Dao. It is a place that can be reached only when a person loses both his "me" and its counterpart, his "opposite." That is, self and other are reciprocal. They form a system in which each entails the other. I cannot be "me" unless I make someone else "other." I cannot be this unless I make someone else that. And I cannot be right unless I make someone else wrong.

In our earlier example, each of the warring parties has done this. The Six says, "You have thwarted me; without you I would be whole and happy!" The Nine retorts, "You have misunderstood and libeled me; without you I would be unblemished and well-respected!" Seen only from his own perspective, each is entirely correct, for all the available evidence supports his vision of how things are. How can they escape their respective viewpoints?

Zhuangzi tells us the escape starts from where "they no longer find *anything* as opposite," that is, when they escape from the entire system that makes self and other necessary. They can only do this when they realize that each of them includes, indeed necessarily implies, the other. That is, the "thwarted one" needs the "thwarting one" and the "libeled one" requires the "libeling one" in order to maintain their identities as thwarted and libeled. Each believes his sense of self proceeds from the other because from the limited perspective of each this is the only possible truth. Yet from the perspective of the Pivot, each one's deepest self is prior to the other's appearance into his life, and from that vantage all individual truths become one great Truth. From their limited perspectives, each has a different opinion of the other, and thus they are opposite. Yet from the perspective of the Pivot, each one's opinion of the other is identical, in that each opinion is made up of a this/that, self/other, right/wrong.

In fact, it is precisely the choice of this/that, self/other, and right/wrong that creates the sense of being thwarted or misunderstood in the first place and from that viewpoint it does not matter much which one is thwarted and which one is libeled for they are both suffering and in need of great compassion both for themselves and for one another.

In earlier chapters, we sometimes pictured each type's point of avoidance standing at a midpoint between two opposites, the type's virtue and vice. In the light of *Zhuangzi's* explanation, however, we can now see that this/that, self/other, right/wrong are not simply sets of two-dimensional lines moving in opposite directions but the circumference of a circle having no beginning or end. In our example, the Six's reaction to feeling obstructed by the Nine triggers the Nine's sense of being criticized by the Six, which leads the Nine to avoid the Six, thereby increasing the Six's sense of being thwarted by the Nine, leading to greater demonization . . . and so on and so on. Not only is each one's *shih* the other's *fei*, but more importantly, each one's *shih* creates the other's *fei* and his own, as well. Yet from within their individual perspectives they cannot understand this. They simply appear as opposites.

From the Pivot's emptiness, however, each can begin to see the other as part of himself. They cannot do this conceptually. That is, they cannot just read the last few paragraphs and say, "Yes, I understand and agree with that." They must actually enter the Pivot. That means putting some space around the usual perception of self and other and sensing the live awareness out of which they emerge. Then and only then they become capable of perceiving the *obvious* which is, "Here stand I, angry and hurt by you, and I am really and truly feeling this. Yet when I look for who is angry and hurting, I cannot find anyone but the unanswerable question 'Who is there?' and therein lies my true suffering. And there stand you, angry and hurt by me, and you are really and truly feeling that. Yet when you look for who is angry and hurting, you cannot find anyone but the question 'Who is there?' and therein lies your greater suffering." As such, we are each the same "false self," visibly hurt and angry. And just as surely are we one "true Self," invisibly witnessing our struggle to justify our false selves and all the suffering that this causes us. In our deepest commonality, we are each present to the world as a "me" who has lost its "I." Underneath that we are each present as the same "I" seeking to be revealed as a distinct "me." We are simultaneously and equally loser and lost, absent and present. We are completely one as *Dao* to *De*, as "that which has presence but no form" to "that which has form but no presence."

From this place, we no longer have to choose between parties. Nor do we have to choose between either nine points of view or ten, between being ephemeral shadows or the eternal spotlight, between many gods or the one and only Absolute. *All* knowledge is based in perspective; there is no such thing as seeing from nowhere. All points of view are true, therefore, each from its perspective. But one point of view is privileged, namely the one that realizes that the view from the still point reveals all myriad happenings and things as one. We do not have to choose between the Many and the One, between the nine points of view or the tenth "true" point of view. The answer to the question "Are there many things or only one?" is "Yes." The phenomenal world of daily life is not just meaningless foam churning over some underlying changeless essence. The point of spiritual work is not to kill the ego so that we can arrive somewhere that has no "where" or "when." The meaningfulness of whatever happens to you or to me is not to be found in some other level of being than the one in which it happens. The meaning of life is not to be found somewhere else at some future moment.

There is a Daoist story about this. A sage once asked, "Since the *Dao* is the most precious reality of all, where could it be hidden so no one could steal it for himself?" The disciple answered, "Perhaps in a remote cave in the farthest mountain." The sage replied that someone could undertake the journey and with luck find it there. The disciple then said, "Perhaps in the depths of the largest ocean." The sage countered that someone who was extremely crafty might still find it there. The disciple eventually gave up and asked for the answer. The sage replied, "The only safe way to hide the most precious thing in the world is to hide it everywhere in the world—in that way no one can remove it for himself."

In other words, the significance of the world is hidden within the world. Such a world may be likened to the heavenly potter's wheel. The periphery is full of hooting, hissing, sniffing, sucking, mumbling, moaning, whistling, and wailing. The center is completely still. Both are necessary in order to fulfill the function of the wheel, which is to *Dao*. Hence, the goal of spiritual transformation is neither the creation of someone who hoots and hisses with elegance and only when called for, nor is it the generation of a perfectly enlightened spirit who lives so far removed from life he is never touched by moaning and wailing. The goal is to be a dancing sage who has simultaneous access both to the chaos, doubt, and constant change of the periphery *and* to the still, boundless creativity of the pivot. Only in this way can one roam truly free within the cage.

Appendix D: Short Annotated Bibliography of Books on the Enneagram

Almaas, A. H. *Facets of Unity: The Enneagram of Holy Ideas.* Berkeley: Diamond Books, 1998. A student of Naranjo and founder of the Diamond Heart approach to spiritual growth. One of the truly original approaches to the Enneagram; often abstract and not easy reading but a unique and deeply spiritual perspective.

Daniels, D. and Price, V. *The Essential Enneagram: The Definitive Personality Test and Self-discovery Guide.* San Francisco: Harper Collins, 2009. Specifically written to help the reader determine his or her type. It offers many practical questions to help you decide between types that at first may seem so similar that you cannot choose between them.

Jaxon-Bear, E. *Healing the Heart of Suffering: Using the Enneagram for Spiritual Growth.* Stinson Beach: Leela Foundation, 1987. Written by a wise teacher who has influenced my own growth and development.

Maitri, S. *The Spiritual Dimension of the Enneagram: Nine Faces of the Soul.* New York: Jeremy P. Tarcher/Putnam, 2000. Another student of Naranjo, Maitri offers a clear and emotionally accessible description of the Enneagram as a spiritual path.

Maitri, S. *The Enneagram of Passions and Virtues: Finding the Way Home.* New York: Jeremy P. Tarcher/Putnam, 2005. A second book with a focus on stumbling blocks encountered in spiritual work.

Naranjo, C., M. D. *Enneatype Structures: Self-Analysis for the Seeker.* Nevada City: Gateways/IDHHB, Inc., 1990. One of the original teachers of the Enneagram in this hemisphere. Clear, readable, practical for self-study from the original source.

Naranjo, C., M. D. *The Enneagram of Society: Healing the Soul to Heal the World.* Nevada City: Gateways Books and Tapes, 2004. Translated from the Spanish, this is the latest offering from Naranjo, who now divides his time between California and South America.

Palmer, H. *The Enneagram: Understanding Yourself and the Others in Your Life.* San Francisco: Harper Collins Paperback, 1991. Clearest and best introductory exposition of the Enneagram as a psychological typology. Probably the best book to start with once you have decided to study the Enneagram.

Palmer, H. *The Enneagram in Love and Work: Understanding Your Intimate and Business Relationships.* San Francisco: Harper, 1995. A second book with useful descriptions of both business and romantic relationships among every possible combination of types.

Riso, D. R. *Enneagram Transformations.* Boston: Houghton Mifflin, 1993. Short collection of prayers/mantras for each type. Has a personal, spiritual tone, more so than some of his earlier works, which to me seem more mental and didactic.

Riso, D. R., & Hudson, R. *The Wisdom of the Enneagram: The Complete Guide to Psychological and Spiritual Growth for the Nine Personality Types.* New York: Bantam Books, 1999. A standard compendium, widely taught. Long on theory, somewhat short on practice.

Rohr, R., & Ebert, A. *The Enneagram: A Christian Perspective.* New York: Crossroad Publishing, 2004. An examination of the Enneagram from a Catholic Christian point of view.

REFERENCES

Ames, R. T. Knowing in the *Zhuangzi*: "From Here, on the Bridge, over the River Hao." In Roger T. Ames (Ed.) *Wandering at Ease in the Zhuangzi*. Albany: State University of New York Press, 1998.

Ames, R. T. & Hall, D. L. *Daodejing—Making This Life Significant—Philosophical Translation*. New York: Ballantine Books, 2003.

Daniels, D. & Price, V. *The Essential Enneagram: The Definitive Personality Test and Self-discovery Guide—revised and updated.* San Francisco: Harper Collins, 2009.

Eliade, M. *Cosmos and History: The Myth of the Eternal Return*. New York: Harper Torchbooks/the Bolligen Library, 1959.

Graham, A. C. *Chuang-Tzû: The Inner Chapters*. Indianapolis: Hackett Publishing Co, Inc. 2001.

Huxley, A. *The Perennial Philosophy*. New York: Harper, 1945.

Jaxon-Bear, E. *Healing the Heart of Suffering: Using the Enneagram for Spiritual Growth*. Stinson Beach, CA: Leela Foundation, 1987.

Jochim, C. "Just Say No to 'No Self'" in *Zhuangzi*. In Roger T. Ames (Ed.) *Wandering at Ease in the Zhuangzi*. Albany: State University of New York Press, 1998.

Ladinsky, D. (Ed.) *The Gift: Poems by Hafiz the Great Sufi Master.* New York: Penguin Compass, 1999.

Lin, D. *Tao Te Ching: Annotated and Explained.* Woodstock: Sky Light Paths Publishing, 2006.

Lusthaus, D. "Aporetics Ethics in the *Zhuangzi*." In S. Cook (Ed.) *Hiding the World in the World: Uneven Discourses on the Zhuangzi*. Albany: State University of New York Press, 2003.

MacKenzie, N. H. (Ed.) *The Later Poetic Manuscripts of Gerard Manley Hopkins in Facsimile*. New York and London: Garland Publishing, 1991. First publication date 1918.

Maitri, S. *The Spiritual Dimension of the Enneagram: Nine Faces of the Soul.* New York: Jeremy P. Tarcher/Putnam, 2000.

Moeller, H. G. *The Philosophy of the Daodejing*. New York: Columbia University Press, 2006.

Neruda, P. *100 Love Sonnets: Cien Sonetos de Amor*, tr. by Stephen Tapscott. Austin: University of Texas Press, 1986.

Ouspensky, P. D. *In Search of the Miraculous*. New York: Harcourt, Brace, and World, 1949.

Palmer, H. *The Enneagram: Understanding Yourself and the Others in Your Life*. San Francisco: Harper Collins, 1991.

Palmer, H. *The Enneagram in Love and Work: Understanding Your Intimate and Business Relationships.* San Francisco: Harper Collins, 1995.

Rilke, R. M. *Die Sonette an Orpheus.* Insel-Bücherei, Nr. 115, 1922.

Riso, D. R. & Hudson, R. *The Wisdom of the Enneagram: The Complete Guide to Psychological and Spiritual Growth for the Nine Personality Types.* New York: Bantam Books, 1999.

Roth, H. D. *Original Tao: Inward Training and the Foundations of Taoist Mysticism*. New York: Columbia University Press, 1999.

Tagore, R. *Gitanjali.* New York: Scribner Poetry, 1997 (originally published in Great Britain by Macmillan and Co., Ltd., 1913).

Slingerland, E. *Effortless Action: Wu-wei as Conceptual Metaphor and Spiritual Ideal in Early China*. Oxford: Oxford University Press, 2003.

Strauss, T. "The Self You *Didn't* Want to Realize." *Vol. 1:Version 2.0.* http://www.tedstrauss.com, 2003.

Winn, M. "Way of the Inner Smile: Self-Acceptance—Tao Path to Inner Peace." http://www.HealingDao.com, 2003.

Whyte, D. *Where Many Rivers Meet.* Langley: Many Rivers Press, 1990.

Whyte, D. *Fire in the Earth*. Langley: Many Rivers Press, 1992.

Ziporyn, B. "How Many Are the Ten Thousand Things and I? Relativism, Mysticism, and the Privileging of Oneness in the 'Inner Chapters'". In S. Cook (Ed.) *Hiding the World in the World: Uneven Discourses on the* Zhuangzi. Albany: State University of New York Press, 2003.

Made in the USA
Monee, IL
12 October 2020

44889588R00120